I GUTCHING

OPENING THE 3RD EYE OF LEADERSHIP

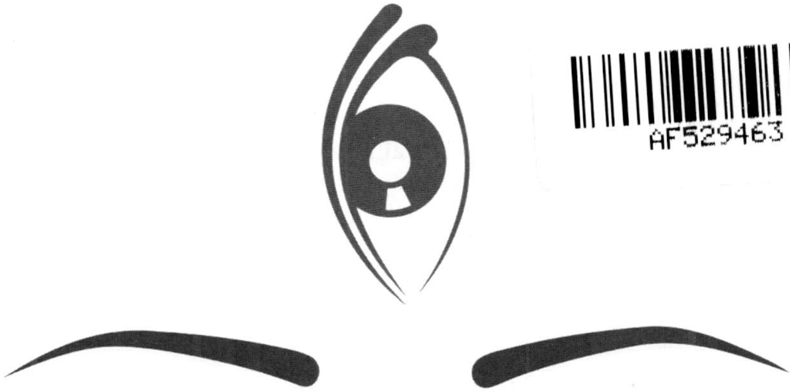

NATURAL INTELLIGENCE is back
Age of CORPORATE CASTEISM is dead
Build your OBSERVATION skills
Know how NATURAL LEARNERS flourish

SEEMA RAGHUNATH

This is a work of Non-fiction. Names of characters have been changed but the story, people, places, events and incidents are real.

First Edition: December 2018

Printed in India

ISBN: 9789387269712

Cover Design: Stuti Jiandani

STORYMIRROR
Stories that reflect you

Publisher: StoryMirror Infotech Pvt. Ltd.
145, First Floor, Powai Plaza,
Hiranandani Gardens,
Powai, Mumbai - 400076, India

Web: www.storymirror.com

Facebook: www.facebook.com/storymirror

Twitter: https://twitter.com/story_mirror

Instagram: https://instagram.com/storymirror

"Give me a blank page, I will show you the magic in me."

Removal of bias is the blank canvas, that brings out true talent in EVERYONE

~ Seema Raghunath

Contents

"I met him many years ago, on a travel when I was put up at a guest house. He was the handyman, man Friday and watch man all rolled into one. He went to school only till the second grade but insisted on speaking whatever English he could remember. "I gutching" was his most frequent usage. Bereft of any grammatical sense, this was his response to confirm, he got what I was saying. "I gutching" meant "I getting" - which in proper English would translate to "I get it"!

The adorable septuagenarian was from the far east of India. He insisted I speak to him in English and not fret over his level of comprehension. In reply to anything I said, he would deliver these two words nodding fervently; an agreement to comfort me that we were still in good communication – still getting each other. He wanted to improve his language skills by understanding and listening better, even if his own speech was weak. The fact that he was still working on it amazed me enormously. He believed it was never too late to learn something new and in Hindi (the local language) said something to the effect of, "Just being open is half the war won against stagnation."

Much wisdom in his words. Stagnation is a natural process too, one that a lot of people enter without realization. It happens when we get overconfident of our skills, enjoy some degree of career success and slowly get recognized for our abilities. **The day conceit kills humility, the continuous leaner also dies.** But if we stay fertile in mind and attitude, much learning will come flying right into our face. It is freely available, provided - we are looking for it.

Our assumptions and prejudices prevent us from truly evolving as we ought to. Almost everyone and everything that happens around us and TO US is saying something. If we manage to read between the lines, we will spade out a thing or two that is worthwhile. There are takeaways in the most banal and simple seeming events, provided one is a natural learner.

To my mother
Jyothi Raghunath,
who is a simple,
virtuous,
intelligent woman.

As a child I remember my mother would sit us down to talk about our legacy, ancestors, relatives, stories and significant events. Each of those stories was telling more than what met the ears. I began to love narratives and soon became an astute listener under her subtle training. Without keen listening one cannot be an observer and perhaps that is why generations ago, storytelling was an important component of intelligence building and education. I owe my mother much for introducing me to the fact that regular LIFE is a vehicle that carries priceless LESSONS.

She harped on the criticality of observation power in assessing situations and people; also because she almost never went wrong with gauging either of them. Her astute assessments were always eyebrow raising. Cleverness is in watching life closely. The people she met, the things that happened in her quiet little world with a handful of friends; shaped and groomed her to use her faculties to their fullest...enough to be one of the most veritable observers I have ever met with sound opinions. She has been a person who evaluates people for how they see things and THINK, not by the tags and status they hold. My first brush with fair evaluations began with my mother's own attitude towards others. Later in life I realized that she is right and that is the best way to see the world.

This book is dedicated to my mother, for helping me see more than myown two eyes can.

Her humble existence and complacent ways never pushed her to seeing the world or suffer the traveler's itch. She always has been one to learn from everything that came free. What I took from observing her was that one can grow from the simplest of sources...if you listen and watch intently. Today when I hear people say they travel the world to learn about life and people - I am forced to remember my mother's humility. I have had to smile and let it pass because the truth and lessons you seek lie at your feet, right there...in home country. Just that many choose not to bend.

The real Voyage of discovery consists not in seeking new landscapes but in having new eyes

- Marcel Proust

What is this book's aim?

This books hopes to reintroduce the value of Natural Intelligence, Natural Leadership and the Natural Learner in the first few pages. It will reveal how the three are interlinked. It aspires to break societal and corporate myths that surround intelligence and capability of talent. This book pushes hard to knock off the biases and detrimental prejudice at the workplace that challenge equal employment opportunities.

It will highlight the casteism we have created and are propounding unwittingly. Workplace casteism is forming a black hole that sucks away really good talent only because they don't fit the bill drawn out by leaders and an HR with poor vision. Along the way the book presents the importance of learning naturally and its many beautiful avenues. The criticality of observation skills in evolutionary leadership and of course...how to evaluate it...to work your way at improving the skill which is seated at the fulcrum of Natural Leadership.

This book will firstly change your views on education and formal learning systems. It will reshape the meaning of learning avenues and introduce you to Travelearning. To get constructive, the topics are designed such that we will first attempt to kill all conditioned bias we hold - then move to working on opening the third eye of the observer. Seven stories of real people and real episodes will provide a platform for evaluating how keen your senses are and your ability to extract meanings.

Your observation will be tested in each simple story here that will toy with your listening prowess. Yes! We listen as we read too! Your OBSERVATION ability is linked to listening, but a different type of listening; a listening that entails the use of all faculties, senses and listening to the unsaid as well. It will show how much you fathom and how far you allow the mind to traverse. Do you reap greater meaning or pick what is at face value? Does much free learning just slip by you?

It will help you evaluate how you connect on two levels - consciousness and sensitivity. By the end of the book, you will have a fair idea of how you stand on Natural Intelligence; the ability to harvest lessons from life and experiences which is the only permanent college we all belong to. Are you just living or are you LIVING and LEARNING? Because only someone who is doing both will grow as an individual and as a professional who is worthy of emulation and rightfully holds the podium of teaching.

"The universe is throwing darts at you all the time. At times it comes from uncanny places and from very ordinary people. People miss it only because their interests and care lie elsewhere. For who harbors the humility to accept the status of being a student will also accept a teacher in any shape or form."

1.

An Introduction to all that is Foundation

The Ancient Kings of India

If there is any testimony in time that presents the indisputable value of common sense, importance of being non judgmental of people's capabilities and the need to be open comes from countless stories in Indian history. A king's kingdom was only as strong or weak as his courtiers were and his army was. But every king knew the importance of heterogeneous talent among courtiers. If you draw parallels between organization and current leaders to kings and kingdoms in what is to follow; you will extract potent ideas.

1) The king never assumed intelligence could be only produced from his kingdom. He stayed open to welcoming the passing man of high intelligence and skills too. Offered him a job, home and status in his court, never treating this new gem as a 'foreigner'.

2) Kings knew the criticality of variety in intelligence, so allowed a range in type of people who assumed roles in the court. A typical Indian court would thus consist of ministers, statesmen, security specialists, artisans, craftsmen, poets, teachers and gurus of various disciplines.

3) Rank was to be earned and not delivered on a platter by virtue of a gurukul (school) someone came from. A student who came from the best school would have to demonstrate his exemplary ability, take on impossible tasks, combat the kingdom's best, and defeat them to earn rank and permanent placement. There were no free lunches then.

4) Equality was a delicate yet prominent thread. At times a master elephant trainer could be revered to hold the same place in court as a clever strategist. Who is to say who is more important than the other? Circumstances choose the moment when a strategist will come of use and at another time a prolific mahout may be

the demand.

5) The Poet and the Treasurer could be paid as equals and that is because remuneration depended on scope, spread and depth of work. A Treasurer has to be the most undisputed on integrity, a great holder of books and capable of forecasting the needs of the kingdom while managing income. However the Poet is the one who transforms thinking, pushes people to ask, imagine out of the ordinary and be liberated enough to also stay creative in every way. You never know when a creative populous will invent something that helps mankind or saves them from the enemy. So a Poet who is teaching youth of the kingdom is as respected as the Treasurer. Respect is not summoned by where you are in the pecking order; but by what you do.

6) Kings at times would notice a deficit of sparky thinkers, knowledge exponents and artisans; that is when announcements would be made inviting the best from everywhere. The competitions and events held were talent showcasing studios where the best could be selected after testing them across hordes of parameters. Talent assessment was unbiased. It would not recognize color of skin, origins and wealth status. When a skill was the need the man could be the child of a scavenger but if he could kill a wild beast by bare hands - he was wanted, honored and treated with the same due respect as any other courtier of high pedigree.

7) Performance was a continuous evaluation. Succession planning took years of observation. If the king has many sons and the firstborn was not necessarily the choice then all sons would be closely observed across pillars of assessment such as:

a) mental agility
b) courage and valor
c) foresight and shrewdness
d) combat skills
e) archery
f) ability to lead people by example
h) People's trust in him.

If these were leadership assessment kings used informally in India circa 5000 and before, makes us wonder why we slip on so many of these today. Blind spots and obnoxious prejudices are banana skins that only skid organizations and leaders into pits of stagnation…if not ruin them in the long run.

Impact Lines

Like the great kings who ran splendid kingdoms and were conscious of the need for strong talent, the need for unbiased acquisition, development and promotion we will focus on **the three impact lines - Talent Acquisition, Talent Assessment and Succession Planning.**

There is no organization that has not suffered on issues pertaining to talent. Good talent is hard to find and it is getting harder as expectations step up substantially. Skills and maturity that were expected out of an employee with four to five years of work experience is what is demanded out of new employees who have zero exposure while expectations are sky high from experienced talent.

Talent Acquisition

But what is worrisome is HOW talent is selected. Unlike wise kings who ran impressive kingdoms, bias and obnoxious prejudice rules this space in present times. It is easy to identify decaying leadership and non-progressive companies by how they advertise jobs. Some state clearly in headers "who can apply". Along with the position that is open will be a mention of three-four colleges they are willing to consider which implies candidates from other universities are officially declared as disposable idiots - unsuitable and thus need not apply at all. Equal Employment Opportunity (EEO) is a wonderful policy but often gets flouted by HR that has poor respect for it. It is the first indication of a company with poor clarity of scruples or having managers who are casteist themselves.

Sometimes it is observed organizations that have leaders as alumni of premium colleges transform into being evangelists for their erstwhile school. They allow entry to only candidates from their own alma mater and can be unabashed in asking Search Companies to follow expectations/their demand. Some are brutally open about it while some others manage their requirement covertly. A world of possibilities is lost in such weak assumptions. Potentially great talent is lost even before they could get to the gates; given no chance for trial or attempt. Whoever attempts has to come from a coterie of pre-approved institutions. **When organizations place their bet on a bloodline based on assumed genetic supremacy than a ratified fact it is Nepotism.** If nepotism was bad and has been stoned by society many times over - how or why is this treated as clean water in the corporate space?

The Human Resources role

As custodians of fair practices, owners of talent acquisition processes, the chastity of people management systems lies with HR. The prevalence of such blasphemy then is like rotten eggs on the face of the entire HR community. It validates inefficiency and in-adeptness to modernize and liberate the workplace from old assumptions and myths.

It clearly indicates need for an HR revolution but many professionals in this space are myopic and fail to see bias as "cardinal sin" because they approved bias as a criteria or pre requisite for so long that they are blind to their own ills. We can't blame them for not being able to see it; if what you see is everywhere, can you still see it?

Conditioning has that kind of effect on the human mind. If garbage is dumped outside your apartment 24/7 for three months, by the fourth month you won't notice it and later still, stop seeing it as garbage altogether, because your eyes shift to more important and meaningful things. In organizations that host incompetent HR, the first sign of inefficiency is the inability to create push back and question bad practices. Where HR is strong they begin to educate leadership to be non conformist to traditional views, drive EEO genuinely, train leaders and managers to assess talent for natural intelligence/values and learning agility and be gate keepers of an OPEN DOOR that welcomes all talent. A equipped HR team need not fret about sifting and sieving talent if they have a good knowledge of how to read people and mechanisms in place to evaluate skills, value orientation along with cultural fitment.

Effect of bias on Talent Assessment and Succession Planning

If attracting talent is shrouded in dark clouds of bias and snobbism, then how can negative impact on Talent assessment and Leadership development be too far behind? Internal employee assessments in many companies are haphazard no matter what fancy tools they claim to use because the Philosophy is either nonexistent or is faulty. Firstly, performance management evaluation parameters are not to be mirrored or marginally modified to turn into leadership assessment parameters. Leadership assessment is for the future therefore current leadership level competencies and behavioral skills cannot be the parameters. For leadership level assessment an individual's next level of competencies comes into frame. As seniority level of leadership assessment grows it moves to more abstract computing - such as Learning Agility, Emotional Maturity, Initiative, Entreprenuerial Spirit and Courage. **These then get driven through, an individual's ability to "Listen, Learn, Leverage and Lift" to get things done.** Competency areas like vision, strategic thinking, influencing ability, customer focus etc add to these pillars, making a system robust.

But even having this does not guarantee fairness and transparency for talent mobilization and career progression. In organizations where labels matter and personal brand is created by additional qualifications from particular schools — the schools show up in the assessment discussion bumping off good candidates. Key talent too gets eliminated for not having a paper that states their brains are stamped and approved by veritable college XYZ. **Succession planning fails when imagined or supposed fitness seated in prejudice outweighs real fitment.** Leaders who will get promoted and who will helm critical roles need not be the most street smart or savvy. They will, however, have credentials that look good on the internet portal and leadership bio.

If we continue on this path of self righteousness and blind sight there is a good likelihood that mature organizations will soon start ear marking companies that ARE close-minded. Close-minded would mean poor decisions, poor demonstration of survival instinct, and predictable talent at the top and poor policies armed with notorious politics that drives survival. So the surviving fittest there would inadvertently be the ones you don't want to touch with a bargepole.

Talent who have lived and survived years in such environment will be equally infected because they too carry the bias virus. The needle of time is pointing towards an evolutionary state where smart organizations stop hiring from outdated shops; scouting for talent from only liberated houses like themselves where the air is free to breathe and only the BEST rise. **Those who are not able to see that casteism will be killed by a bigger casteism to come, have tunnel vision that will cost them much.**

BIAS, Prejudice and Bad Programming

We are programmed beings

Everything is institutionalized today. Without formal process, formats and templates, we are lost. We have begun to attach merit to only what is predictable and is a methodical form of learning. What is free, what is at our disposal is rejected for being just that – free and available. We desperately need to change our attitude if we wish to be virile learners; unadulterated by modern day structured concepts of progress. There is beauty in simplicity and unless we go back to discovering it, we will forever lose that path.

"In the ideal world, one must be capable of leading self as both teacher and student simultaneously."

Brand consciousness

This has afflicted the human mind so much and so far, that most are blind to accept lessons outside of a reputed school that holds desired rating or has been mentioned often in media. When we follow a formal discipline, we learn what everyone else is learning too. There is nothing differential or outstanding. To be able to represent on paper one fine day what was put into your head thorough the year, pretty much sums up formal learning. The exemplary learner is who was learning from a library, from a job on the side, from struggles and perils of life, from overcoming personal challenges or from watching other. What this does is that it adds a few more colors to the personality than just grades. Yet the takers are few because there are no rewards for self learning without accreditation.

However the attachment of brand makes sense where formal learning systems are sought for streams like STEM – Science, Technology, Engineering and Math. It is completely credible when one is picking up functional knowledge and expertise in certain streams where structured learning is especially potent because of the exposure to masters who turn into teachers at such universities. For example: medicine, engineering, architecture, catering schools etc bring in the very best to be lead anchors of programs to make the courses veritable. Where this bias becomes superfluous is when it is a graduation in general streams or general management. These are areas where the natural learner flowers better than someone in a structured system.

Regardless of what brand one picks up formal education from, leaning outside of school via all simulations requires you to rely on your ability to turn into your own teacher. What you learn thus is because of your inherent observation skills and craftiness to convert it into lessons. Being your own trainer and faculty is harder than being a recipient or student.

The receiving end can absorb only what the giving end gives. So unless you are a good teacher for yourself this journey towards self evolution can be a very hard one.

Self DISCOVERY

Once you learn to own your own school, be your own teacher and run your own classes – it is a skill learnt for a lifetime. This trophy talks tall of your capacity to groom your mind. The best of colleges today brag of using self discovery as a process that is most enlightening and contributory to development. The irony of our lives in the 21st century is that we accept this in brochures and prospectus of fancy colleges not realizing that is the eternal truth and has been so for all this while.

The importance of self discovery and self learning is not disputed – its source is. We fail to heed the words of an ordinary man only because he is not allocated the position of being a veritable professor or someone who holds a PhD. Natural and simple always comes first. But our attachments are so classist that we have rubbished the rules of the cosmos. It is futile to assume formal learning is the ONLY center seat of education yet it is tough to convince people to propel forth on an aggressive path of self tutoring.

Life - the first GURU

Once man has learnt to speak, read and write, much of REAL learning that shapes personality and character happens in what we see, experience, hear, listen, absorb and imbibe at an individual level. It is therefore not uncommon to meet people who are highly educated and supposedly refined but still find them rough. They may display poor personal values and questionable choices besides some obvious uncouthness as well. On the other hand it is highly possible that there in a remote village and sitting under a tree, is a rustic man in a dusty garb, decorated by people's attention and respect. His words are so profound hundreds huddle to listen to him – to be motivated and to learn. No designer suits, no stuffy concepts, no image consciousness – he is perhaps simplicity personified. The only offering he brings is real time knowledge that is factual, inspiring and practical. And it is also so commonly seen in countries like India that some day such a man turns evangelist, transforming lives and destinies till men in suits from the best of organizations seek his counsel to direct/teach/guide or show them the way. There is no Harvard or Oxford behind his name but there is a much bigger brand in himself… one that grew by embracing life's college.

"The world has seen enough nobodys rise and march mankind into a new destiny by the sheer power of their conviction and the strength of their passion. Yet we choose to believe the harbinger of change mandatorily will come from a place of much repute because intelligence without certificates…is virtually impossible."

Rise of the Corporate Brahmins Breaking bias. Opening doors

No man who worships education has got the best out of education... Without a gentle contempt for education no man's education is complete."
-G.K. Chesterton

This chapter comes from a blog I wrote in the year 2011 which is why it will be presented in first person.

"I am not against formal education at all but certainly miffed by how we have made it the discriminating factor. Discrimination has gone so far that we discount an individual's natural intelligence unless it is vetted by some external body known to house students of a certain IQ. We discredit the PRAGMATIC learner who learns from life and seeks avenues for learning; who may be finest observer there is and is committed to lifelong self development and change. We prefer someone who has got the seal of approval from a certain campus to take that chance with hiring them. This is how the rise of the corporate brahmins begins. It is a bunch of people dunked in bias and prejudice who confidently splash their classist attitude across an organization's hiring, retaining and development policy and process, making it one terribly murky place that gives rise to more such corporate brahmins.

I coined the term, the "Corporate Brahmin" in 2011, right in the middle of a heated debate with someone who was pro hiring from only India's top four campuses. He presented a view point that sidelined the possibility that good talent could exist holding a simple degree. He was unwilling to acknowledge good talent could possess a sea of knowledge from earlier job experiences armed with ample common sense. The blindness with which some people of power design laws and policies can infringe employee rights, fairness and equality squat in the face! Being a custodian of equal employment opportunity and talent management practices I have fought tooth and nail to keep this space devoid of discrimination and bigotry. Everything looks yellow to a jaundiced eye and the power of preventing such disease lies with professionals who don critical role in HR thus.

I had to strategize argument lines to try to reason with such vociferous leaders. What saddened me however was to find myself outnumbered in most groups that debated the subject. You can bet your bottom dollar in time there will always be ample people in a room who agree with such discrimination only because it is not vehemently labelled as BIAS. In such meetings I met some people of power whose sole determination of good, intelligent, capable talent was if they came from X or Y schools/management institutes. Not just words, their facial expressions and gestures too liberally dismiss other candidates the same way you'd feel about a Pizza left uncovered overnight. It is times like these that helped me develop the skill of holding a poker face while my blood is actually boiling.

Many would not be open to consider B-schools outside the A-list, leave alone regular colleges or streams. Often their own alma mater slithered in as one that is in the esteemed club. They'd make sweeping comments and irrational assumptions around candidate potential, abilities and even leadership capabilities of very pragmatic learners only because their MBA was not full-time or because the college was in a small town.

Questions without answers

Why is General Management being made out to be a Genetic Science equivalent? How confounding will MBA application be at the workplace in a job where functional expertise is mastered already? It is not like they will deconstruct a human protein and label it wrongly; thereby changing classification which alters the destiny of genetic medicine for decades to come — causing fatalities along the way.

MBA — how life altering is this as subject? And how vividly different will the content be for different schools? *If there subject on a platter which is the copyright of only the best?* Or will frameworks or models of reputed researchers change depending on curriculum? How ground shaking will it be if a candidate didn't make it to the top 33 percentile or did only a one year course? If the person is a great natural learner with good years of work experience under his/her belt, they would have equipped themselves with all useful and prolific skills as it is...with or without an MBA. Then how does an MBA make a candidate better when the course does not really touch the person behind the professional? Having seen a few rare colleges that actually offer unique MBA's that work intensely on the human being as they do on the professional I can safely say those are seriously stellar. Rest are plain vanilla using a dozen sexy names to sell themselves to the silly.

Without meeting talent, how in the world can anyone claim certainty of quality and confirmation of supreme beings in all the three hundred who annually graduate from a particular stone building just because it has a tough entrance exam and is prestigious? How can you bestow super talent status to anyone without a formal judging, gauging process and be okay with a lame "it is well established"?

International complications

As if local comparators and stack ranking of schools was not enough to reject good talent, in would enter foreign colleges to sprinkle rock salt on raw wounded disputes. The arguments in such strategic Succession Planning meeting would often leave Indian campuses to land us in UK or traverse the US campuses aggressively. Being the self appointed defense attorney crusading for all those thousands and millions of wonderfully potent talent in the world who didn't have the good fortune, conditions or inclination to get a seat, pay the fees and actually survive that education has been a tough road for me but the findings on bias is more than astounding.

The Internal Classification begins

When A-listed colleges are the pre-designated hiring grounds, even B or C grade Business schools get conferred "second class" ranking. Organizations that talk openly, giving voice to such classifications for hiring/talent acquisition, automatically move many of their incumbent employees to being second grade organization citizens. The rule applied to get someone from outside will also apply on who is inside the house now.

In a heavily partisan environment like this, those without any school worthy of mention end up as the "cattle class" though they are never called out so. I am caustic to the degree of third degree burn on this subject, because prejudice has ruined many a good civilizations, communities and people; it also can destroy companies by eating into environment, climate and culture, which usually shows up in poor Employee Survey Scores (ESS) and Competitive edge in Performance and Business success. Organizations that are stooping under poor ESS need to turn the mirror towards them instead of the employee for a bit - ask if they have been Corporate Brahmins. **Organizations cannot mar opportunity and a fighting chance for good talent because of some wicked out dated dogma. Hurting**

wholesome *talent and denting their careers is not an organization prerogative... unless it is running a sweatshop. Organizations with poor business results also need to look at how far their Corporate Brahminism has shunned the truly innovative, radical thinker from moving into leading roles.*

The term

My usage of the term the Corporate Brahmin has ruffled many feathers because of what it really means. However this term here is restricted to driving home the concerns that surround visible casteism. All casteism emanates from the assumption of a few people's superiority complex over others. What is being practiced by corporate organizations is a similar discrimination where large numbers of unwitting employees are coerced into believing the system is fair and well thought through when it is subjugating and classist. The term Corporate Brahmin is not to be seen as castigation or any form of judgment on the present state of social affairs in the Indian society.

Vedic India was a time of much intellectual growth and maturity in the Indian civilization. Vedic ideology governed society then. Hinduism as a religion was crafted into a shape and form many thousand years later. While Hinduism is hinged on principles from the Vedic age, some dilutions happened along the way. In Vedic India the varna system took birth with a noble intention of allowing people to take on roles in the community based on skills, competency and merit. Who could learn, read, memorize the complex sanskrit scriptures and eventually teach the next generations became Brahmins. There was no caste at this juncture. A person could thus change varna depending on his skills and abilities.

However, over time varna became representative of a caste. Something that is predetermined at birth. This system rationalized the process at first by peddling it as something that was for the welfare of the society. By evaluating potential of people by bloodlines, they will excel at what they are ordained to do was the logic they gave to themselves and others. It eventually became a system that throttled the other castes that didn't have the ranking needed to have a say or contribute to decisions. The people closest to the temple – the brahmins began to rule the roost and over time became arrogant controllers of the community. Not that there were no poor, malnourished brahmins – like in all society that has a classist history, few scamper and make it to the top leaving even their own brethren behind to suit their plans for power.

The leads designed the divide themselves and benefited from it over the centuries to come. Invasions made the issues far graver. People in India know the

Hindu caste system has not been kind to some layers of society but such casteism is well known across the world just that colonizers drummed the ills of our society to use it as a weakness only their ruling can fix. The irony of education is that Indians were taught about how caste system was inhuman by the British education system while it nowhere had the gumption to accept its own cancers.

In old England, the nobles and those credited social ranking clearly severed themselves from the poor. The community of human settlement did not even dare to share space. The poor and downtrodden were thrown out to live on the outskirts of towns and cities, reducing them to generations of poverty, sickness and being outcastes. The more the severance worse the facilities, access to health care, basic needs, fire, food, shelter and education. The caste system of Britain was centered around wealth. Over time last names became indicative of the placement of the person. How different? Not at all. This goes to prove that casteist thinking did its duty to kill human societies world over from the sugarcane fields of the US that carries sordid history of black slavery and white man supremacy to Britain to modern India. What the world today narrates however is the evil caste system of India while most others shove their own casteisms under a carpet of being civilized. No community is truly civilized till it first acknowledges the dirt in their own backyard which is why I chose to give this garbage of the corporate space an Indian terminology than just keep it global or neutral. **Courage is not in defiance or denial ....it solely lies in acceptance of the truth.**

India's tryst with casteism

A classist society can divide its people by wealth or knowledge but a divide is evident. England broke the back of its society by wealth evaluators while ancient India did that on the basis of knowledge and skills. Nobody around the world is happy about how ignoramus and hideous our ancestry has been – all we know is that we don't want to repeat any of it. **It has taken modern human society centuries to overthrow the nuisance and declare equal rights for all...but the ugly head of that monster has been raising its head at workplace – yet we ignore it because nobody has declared its menace.**

If you look closely, all logic we use today in context to hiring from certain watering holes of knowledge is just the same casteism, like the brahmins constructed thousands of years ago. They said it will be the best way to segregate good quality people for good roles and likewise, the leaders of today state the same bias in their arguments. It took India thousands of years to break free from the iron grip of this horror, which is why it is hard for me to watch Corporate Brahmins replicating the same things unwittingly in the corporate space. **Education fails when its application is unsuccessful. Application fails because the mind is working on conditioned thinking; or following trends while being incapable of asking the WHYs and the WHY NOTs.** My argument that people who learn from the walk of life, who are pragmatic change agents are equally potent; validates its stand every time a person without many frills claims a coveted mantle.

Gets worse at Leadership Levels

Ignoring someone's success over decades as managers and leaders is not just insulting but is also reflective of the assessors' degree of visual impairment. At leadership positions we are talking of people with years of experience, wins, plus failures — all proven and documented. Why should anything else matter except their ability to think, DO and lead business plus people. Campus comes back to haunt careers, decades after the smell of their hallways are forgotten. Something is gravely wrong with the corporate space if we think professionals with work records that spanned two-three decades should still be attached to their schools.

Real Case

Logic says that when it comes to career progress and leadership evaluation, track record of results, orientations and behaviors should govern judgment. In one meeting we were discussing a fantastic talent; one who cumulatively across years had proven to be the most potent among contemporaries. He was a declared as a key talent. Then some wise guy mentioned — "But he does not have an MBA". It was discussed like it was a legit handicap! That one subject was beaten like a dead dog for an hour in a 20 minute Talent review but the consensus group considered it worthy discussion to bust time norms. This spot on his profile made him a lesser man. The result was that the group declared "He should be sent off to do a course right away from Y University" the way chemotherapy saves a man. All my teeth grinding and argument only resulted in my having shorter teeth and a hoarse voice, but nothing changed in their mindsets. I failed completely at making others realize that the school of learning is just like God – it's everywhere. That it is unfair to state learning agility, intelligence or radical absorption is in the negative just because someone didn't go to a certain college which is on a secret list, sitting in YOUR pocket.

But REAL learners are deemed too middle class to be allowed a chance to fight for chairs. Just like the logic of monarchy bloodlines. An idiot born to the king will be a better king than a peasant with wit and skills. Any view that is so dipped in singular assessment based on brand value cannot be accurate or even marginally just. And there sits in such obtuse prejudice, our biggest loss. We stifle natural intelligence and right brain thinkers who are the epicenter of creativity. All intelligent people need not be creative but all creative HAVE TO be intelligent. When will this rationale seep into our consciousness? The pragmatic natural leader only needs a level playing field and not special polices or considerations.

"There is Pride and Prejudice in education casteism but no Sense and Sensibility."

True leadership could be anywhere – but it gets killed by Corporate Brahmins

There are so many leaders without a snazzy degree who today own companies and lead thousands of people worldwide that it would be safe to say that every country, every state, every city has someone like that. Their names, some known and some unknown, changed the world we live in. I won't bring names with history and the story of their evolution because social media has covered many of them as it is. These are people who learnt more than any school could ever teach and who taught more than most teachers could.

DO NOT judge a book by the cover is more than just an adage. Had these successful pioneers worked with warped leaders, despite being the best observers and learners from life, perhaps their spirit would have taken a beating or someone that blind would have clipped their wings. **The relentless spirit of such learners and doers is that they break free when the environment gets too claustrophobic and that is when they find themselves and the direction to head in.**

The loss of such potential is "felt" by an organization but never recognized. Such people are appreciated by diamond hunters and liberal organizations, who know the value of who they have met. Sadly they are far few and too in between. The rise in corporate brahmins will bring ruin unless we nip it in the bud. A work environment cramped by biases, prejudice and the jaundiced eye can't be good for a vast majority. Potential leaders are everywhere tucked away into dark corners. They have been dumbed into believing the world has no place for them unless they toe in line and do what is expected so the gateways of entry open for them. Many tire trying to fit in and most watch the ebb of their ambition because corporate society is a plagued space. As it stands today - it takes a keen eye and a willing mind to discover these hidden jewels.

The world constitutes of more ordinary people with extra ordinary ability than the elitist with extraordinary ability. The Corporate Brahmins are blind as a bat for as long as they chose to ignore this fact.

Every sighted problem deserves a solution as soon as it is uttered if that be helped. And now that a corporate nuisance has been called out, it is important to dwell a bit on possible solutions. It is highly unproductive to rake up an issue lustily, if its answers are too confounding.

In the case of campus hires or those fresh to the workplace, companies who are progressive could design a pre-hiring process that encapsulates a water-tight filtration process. One that is a combination of online tests, written tests or external exams without asking for information on nationality, gender or college/school they completed their last course from. This kind of neutrality will serve as a common filter that does not sieve out applicants basis school of graduation. When it sieves, it will evaluate intelligence, cognitive abilities, value orientation, capabilities and skills. The mandated tests could be hosted on company websites or through staffing partners or even on campus location. This communicates to the external market, that the company is one NOT to have reservations or quota for only a certain type of school. It demonstrates Equal Employment Opportunity as a belief system and also as practice. The world has moved to counting "Say-Do" ratio to form brand opinion. With a process such as the one mentioned above it will be a case of, "May the best woman or man win — minus any discriminatory criteria".

Business schools, if they are so sanguine of their produce then there ought to be no resistance to allow a fair fight with the majority that didn't walk in their corridors of learning. Organizations can make tests for managers and above competitive, by designing them to mirror competency, skills and behaviors required to survive One day in THAT Job. It will make assessment centers absolutely aligned to the job profile; evaluating both functional skills where it's applicable and behavioral compliments as well. Or bring out a list of Knowledge, Skills and Attributes with calibrators, using Behavioral Event Interviewing (BEI) style. This would require keeping education qualifications outside of the purview of first level assessment for general management roles.

For leadership positions, an erstwhile school cannot be the fulcrum of selection. The history of performance, experience, exposure, adaptation, successes and leadership stories by then are stacked up to the roof. Such data is the most veritable data of relevance. Meeting or interviewing them face to face has to be the crux of selection besides evaluating talent for cultural fitment, VALUES and ambition. **A good school in such cases would only be cherry on an awesome, authentic cake....not the cake itself.**

Not creating Nemesis!

My own experience having led Talent Development and OD roles brought me face to face with many strange sightings. Produce from the best colleges expect strategy jobs, visionary roles, end to end project and people responsibility even while their experience is nil. I have been witness to candidates who came from some of the best schools in the world whose sense of entitlement would made a music diva look tame. The delta between organization expectation and readymade packaged leadership potential from colleges lies in Character – Values – Behavior. **The day educational institutions give this a 50% weightage along with 50% to academic scores during admission is when we will see a world that has a produce from formal systems who are truly worth the hype.**

But for those who didn't get the chance to be in such institutions, nothing much is lost. Life is the best college there is. Anyone who can milk life correctly, can beat the best out of any college – anytime – any day — hands down. This however is an art and also a practiced skill; one that lies in heightened senses making one forever stay as the constant observer. A person like this connects, links and co-links so seamlessly that all theory, practicals, concepts and hypothesis will unfold outside of text books – in the real world where everything matters and is tangible.

Institutions of repute will continue to hold impressive stature not because of the wisdom of a robust philosophy or change in system but because a lot of them have some of the finest teachers the world has to offer. These colleges also use formats and contemporary content which make their teaching system flawless. However, their brilliance will shine through when their system shows diversity. Diversity in TYPE of intelligence. Intelligence is not a one way street made of just scores. **Creativity is intelligence that loved to design. Radical thinking is intelligence that dared to be different. Experiment is intelligence playing permutation combination. Pragmatism is intelligence that gave a thrashing to theory. Intelligence exists in many shades and forms.** To think intelligence is best judged by scores is the worst mistake we make. Because who scores may not necessarily possess imagination, courage, vision, passion and energy to DO; then what do you do?

The world has been proven wrong on homogeneity being the ideal state. Heterogeneous groups think better and deliver greater results. When all formal education and the corporate spaces change ideologies to begin to mirror IDEO, the Californian design company is when we can say we have arrived in the new era of Fair Practices and Best output. IDEO enfolds in its talent group diverse people with or without degrees; but with abundant natural intelligence, curiosity, character, motivation, CREATIVITY and structured discipline. IDEO broke the shackles of thinking in 1991. Some companies adopted their view of the world and people capacities. Like Google…and we all know how well they did. Yet we are moving at snail's pace in that direction of being less classist and more open.

That said, we cannot nullify the contributions of good universities nor suggest their placement in the overall grooming system to be weak. Nor dismiss the modern and competitive education such schools present or the athletic curriculum and pace they offer. What we need to do is to trigger much needed modern thinking and outlook towards talent and own up our responsibility as change agents. All universities and great schools of name stand secure in their place of social worship and contribution to economy, to organizations and the community, especially if they adapt regularly, knowing the shape and form of talent need that has changed.

We need to bring focus onto the innumerable talent who are intelligent, above the average curve, but didn't end up in schools of repute owing to circumstances. People with much promise who continue sharpening their saw from other grounds which is why the alumni of distinguished houses will still end up locking horns with them at board rooms and discussion meetings. The self taught are no less if not better. The clash of the titans very often is among those holding formidable college tags against who have no bearings of a higher campus name; yet offering the same resistance, power, knowledge, and sense.

The world has not always changed and been reformed by the best of intellect that came from the best of schools. It is time we open stage to pure potential that can change the course of tomorrow — and that can happen only if we give TRUE TALENT, a fair chance. Universities and colleges need to own up the responsibility of removing class consciousness that somehow seeps into the psychology of their students making them undeserving of snootiness and the sense of entitlements they carry with them as newbies at the workplace. Humility never goes out of fashion especially not when one is still a learner. Besides **the success of their students lies in whether they know that their toughest opponent out there is probably NOTHING LIKE THEM**.

Jingoism in this case is the extreme attachment to the belief that a school or university is the be all and end all of talent production. Such dogmatism by leaders is a wasted voice if it is not supported by unsurpassable produce generated by the said schools. The best of schools will release each year what they call, "The Brains that will lead Business". But those among that lot who are not great observers, not good at listening beyond words, who have not shaped their character and who won't learn from avenues other than what is formal – are not really competition at all. The real tool – the only weapon is CONTINUOUS LEARING. And with that, some academically simpler others, could get far ahead, sped up by their prehensile minds and agility to change.

This perspective mentioned here, will not be so pleasant for those who have personally anguished flipping pages of a hundred text books, wrote forty exams a year only to be a notch ahead of the thousands outside the walls of their college, only to be told, "The others" have not been vanquished permanently". If anyone thinks a peer from a likewise college is the only competition to anticipate – they couldn't be more wrong. Honest realities can temporarily stun but have to be accepted as fact.

"The others" are the majority that roam the world and every workplace has ample of them. Not all are potent but a good percentage are strong contenders. Contenders without ornate convocations. Safe to say not all who stayed outside of prestigious colleges will be aggressive at self learning to pose as serious a threat. **There are sufficient seemingly ordinary ones who have the gumption and voracious appetite to learn from floating free radicals of information**. It would be right to say careers will not be a cake walk despite honors' from a great academia if one is not competitive and all absorbing all the way.

"It is about time we change, and change fast. Stay abreast of this phase of evolution that demands unusual solutions, from unusual minds. Unusual minds can be in unusual places. To find them we just need to be open."

2.

Natural Intelligence, Natural Learners and Natural Leaders

CHAPTER 1: NATURAL INTELLIGENCE

Why are people with NI the anchors of organizations and human society

Natural Intelligence

Natural intelligence as it suggests, is the instinctive inborn common sense driven outlook, approach, perspective and attitude of an individual. Natural intelligence thus is the most ancient style of survival that does not rely on formats, templates, theories and designs crafted by academia. A person of natural intelligence could thus be a village postman, a manager at a bank, a business leader running an empire, a small town primary school teacher or a house wife.

Natural intelligence does not select its host like formal education based qualifications do. Yet it is the most formidable of intellectual capabilities to ever be found and experienced. A person with abundant natural intelligence is the fastest learner. They stitch things quickly. Ask many tough questions that usually crop up from experts. They are married to common sense so sincerely their ability to see the big picture, distant vision and view all things holistically is seamless. Natural intelligence is linked to the natural learner who very often is also a natural leader.

Why is Natural intelligence (NI) hard to assess?

Natural intelligence is hard to quantify and evaluate unless the person evaluating is high on natural intelligence themselves, besides NI does not respond to plain Jane IQ tests. A person of natural intelligence may in fact not score well in designed IQ evaluations. Their territory is way too different from programmed thinking and reasoning.

The assessment of NI will factor:

1) Ability to work using common sense

2) Spontaneous data collection of what is relevant followed by sorting skills

3) Instinctive capability of identifying gaps and possible plugs for the same

4) Comprehension of challenges with the degree of their constraints

5) Willingness to consider range of options/solutions from what is related, adjacencies and even unrelated

6) Ability to stay attached to end objectives/goals without resorting to mindless detours

7) Design and implement pragmatic solution journey's creatively.

Once the above is initiated you can see why assessing natural intelligence is hard for most people especially at interviews where you barely get an hour to get to know the talent. Assessing NI is largely possible at the workplace when studying teams and gauging leadership potential which provides many long term observation opportunities. It still demands exceptional ability to study, note, and identify the indicators of natural intelligence. Some of the best situations to assess natural intelligence is when unexpected issues arise, there is crisis, challenges in an area nobody is well versed in…these are times and conditions when the one with natural intelligence will 1) Show up voluntarily 2) Start demonstrating his or her NI instinctively.

VALUE of talent with NI in organizations

Talent with NI show the propensity to survive and thrive against all odds of market condition, industry shape or stature of profitability and performance. They are not necessarily who we term as Key Talent. Key Talent are who will do well in this industry, move to another unrelated and do well there too because they are intrinsically motivated and have superior control over skills and competencies. But not all Key Talent need have Natural Intelligence and not all with NI will get listed as Key Talent in organizations.

Those with NI lead as the moment demands and have the courage to explore outside of well trodden templates. People with natural intelligence may be rule breakers, outliers and not necessarily fitting into the Cultural - Political set up of a structured organization so get booted out of such assessments unless strong leaders can tell who these people really are and find ways to bring out the best. Folks with NI find it humiliating to use, apply, accept anything without independent study. They study to convince themselves of the idea or process. They take pride in their ability to Think Differently and DO Differently. They are the true human capital

- real assets to any organization.

Time to Break the biggest GLASS CEILING

Organizations and HR who have not given sufficient importance to NI which is the most critical element of leadership, prefer to demand degrees and educational qualifications; preferably from premier institutes, assuming natural intelligence comes with convocation ceremonies. There is a whole world of exceptional talent that has been smothered by corporate assumptions and biases. The assessment of talent needs to be linear. If it is bi focal with one lens on qualification and the other on the talent themselves...those who don't possess the qualification to impress fall off the range of vision. When the talent is not even within the range of view, how do you suppose they will be explored, invested in and groomed for full potential?

What we need in our current age and time with all the threats that prick economy, society and the human race in general is the breaking of this GLASS CEILING to usher in the best there is, regardless of prejudice which horribly adds challenge to the existing dearth of talent we see. Today, many backward organizations and seriously backward leaders both in business and HR follow the practice of declaring certain positions as reserved although they don't use the term "reserved". It is reserved for Talent from XYZ university — Batch year 123 to 456. Unevolved" companies show no qualms in proclaiming their bias on popular job portals or demanding it from Search firms they retain or hire to close positions. Discrimination is starkly sitting there in every such advertisement, every such creation of job mandate which assumes only someone from a given college list with given year of graduation can perform with exemplary results and hold Natural Intelligence.

If there is a shred of doubt — Let's clear it

If parenting rules were to be applied to leadership then you will see beautiful overlaps. Same rules apply in both places when shaping children or developing teams and talent is concerned. If you had two children of which one is academically a genius, scores the best and is considered an outstanding student who brings home many medals and trophies while the other is a marvel at being your sounding board, co-planner, a resolute philosopher and adviser then who would you place as valuable over the other?

As a parent you will balk to utter something discriminatory. That is because both are talented — differently. Both are using intelligence but it is demonstrated in different arenas. Interestingly, if you told them to swap places and excel in each other's domains — both might either do just so- so or even fail. As a parent what we do is RESPECT natural intelligence and ability each child brings. We hone the natural interests in them to nurture and help them flower; yet when we move our zone to running or leading organizations suddenly prejudice and bias begins to lead us. Why?

The outcome of Breaking this Glass Ceiling

One of the biggest positive outcomes is that it will allow the emergence of talent that has TRUE natural intelligence. Anyone with strong NI will get a fair chance. They could be from prominent formal colleges or not. But the removal of this prejudice which is a mandatory criteria today for many (some practicing it openly while some discreetly) means all talent will get treated as equal. For as long as this bias stays, talent from prestigious universities will be seen as talent while those who didn't pursue such avenues will linger on as only resources.

Is that the maturity we wish to see and display in this age and time? Identification and empowerment of people with natural intelligence means enormous transformation alongwith positive change in talent selection, development, retention and career progression too. The question is...are we ready?

Chapter 2: Natural Leader

The effortless Leader who leads people and businesses into strength

Who is a Natural Leader?

Natural Leaders: The reference here indicates to people who show an innate ability to stand out in a crowd, lead others and be consistent influencers. They manifest signs of revolutionary thinking, are instinctive change agents, carry conviction in their beliefs and most IMPORTANTLY have the ability to make that energy infectious. **Natural leaders have the courage to use their knowledge to trigger right thinking that propounds positive change regardless of opposition or being affected by their hierarchical standing.**

Natural leaders are not necessarily taught, coached and readied into assuming leadership roles — they often just end up taking on responsibilities, executing them without a flinch while other people readily queue up to share their vision. They may have sought qualifications that add stars to their lapel but most of who and what they are, is already a part of their DNA and personality. Formal education only further sharpens an already sharp mind. But if they didn't have brag worthy institutions to grant them the honor of being their produce…a natural leader still would be as strong alone, as they would be carrying the name of a brand on them. **Later in their career and life, you will see they begin to shape a personal brand and image that is almost entirely independent of the company they work for or the profession they are in. Such leaders hone an image that is "formidably attractive" by just being themselves**. Natural leaders have another peculiarity - they are intensely mindful of their strengths and the strengths of the people they meet because they live and work by only the application of strengths not fussing over drawbacks.

So what makes Natural Leaders?

The Mind. Natural leaders have the strength of mind that is truly exemplary. This strength requires further understanding because it is not the predictable strength of usual competencies and skills that we often see or talk about. Nor is mind's strength here to be confused with the ability to listen or comprehend or store or reproduce which is nothing but a plain cookie cutter academically groomed mind at work.

The ability to stay connected to all senses and instantaneously pull and use sensory memory stashed away across all the years of life and living — that is what makes a Natural leader so unique. Natural leaders carry a repository of data that they can dip into anytime and relevant information is thus available at their beck and call.

Knowledge is their strength. They are holders of a rich, vast and private library. Universal knowledge of all that they read, sensed, witnessed, experienced, solved, touched, realized, grew out of, adopted, adapted, accepted and adjusted is stored in the vault of their brain. This stashing away is like a filing process that happens in their sub conscious mind; however available for the conscious mind to bring forth when a suitable time permits/demands the reference. Harder than it sounds but easily performed by such leaders; often making them the envy of those who are at the receiving end of their reasoning and artful arguments. A lot of their confidence arises out of having challenged themselves and pitting themselves against other intellectual Titans.

Wide attention span

In a given moment they show the capacity to be attentive to umpteen different activities/actions/subjects which is them basically deploying one of their senses on each job. Example: Ravit is a natural leader. He is talking to his manager and has to listen intently on the plan for a new agreed solution that will handle a current problem. But a customer who has come with a complaint is also narrating issues few desks away. Keeping track of words, tone, body language and subtle hints from both — manager and customer will happen harmoniously although the two events are independent of each other.

Processing emotions is also unique because emotions get compartmentalized. Therefore an antiseptic view of possible solutions happens. Ravit, while he works on addressing manager demands, also needs to know if his team member is handling the meeting with the customer well enough or needs help. He instinctively assigns a part of his mind to keep an eye on the reportee. Looking for signs of distress, position of body's incline, gestures, confidence of hand movements, reference to documents etc to study how that meeting is going and also stays involved, sensible, practical in what he is attending to. Natural leaders don't feel the strain in dividing their mind across subjects because they have trained themselves for years on how to do it without affecting the space and the people they are physically present with. At any point when the pressure gets too far with this balancing, Ravit will declare one item more important than the other to do justice and handle things as they come because his confidence is something that is ingrained.

Their Values

Coupled with strong values and conviction for each of their values, they stand comfortable in who they are, why they are the way they are — at times unapologetic. The reason they seem formidable is because they can be vehement drivers who can flick away speed breakers in the form of things that come in the way and people who oppose or turn into impediments. The more masterful among natural leaders can ruffle many people in early years of exploration when they have not yet learnt how to deploy their knowledge to influence others. As years go by natural leaders struggle less with work and output. As reliable bankable performers they would have earned a name. They may however at times struggle with getting people unlike themselves to see the light of day or encourage the acceptance of their style.

How they use TIME differently

One needs to remember a Natural Leader need NOT be a leader with a given position of high rank and stature. Some don't make it that far if their temperament and ambition has not been complimenting or they are stuck in the wrong place at the right time. Regardless of where they are in life, time is treated with respect and much attention. One marked difference between ordinary people and Natural leaders is their awareness of Time itself. The reverence for the passing of time, the people they give their time to and who are occupying it, is important to them.

At some subliminal level it is a conscious realization of time being a priceless commodity — the most precious one we possess. This also explains why they treat people who are sharing time with them — with great regard. Time is like a capsule that traps us with some individuals in a moment, situation, event or condition. It allows the play up of ideas along with emotions making a story happen. **Natural**

leaders are like directors and cinematographers who know what scene this is, who is playing what role here, is it appropriate to fade or rise in the given scene, must they let things flow without interception or lead; and amidst all this seem to also be writing down the critique's synopsis of the play. The registering is done. Time is attached to people and all the variables in it. The sequence of events and outcomes are virtually penned to the extent they know the triggers of and what the twists were. So what makes them collect so much? Note so much? That's because for them everything is knowledge. The Natural Leader is a Natural Learner and that is why everything however insignificant seeming, will and is getting filed.

Leadership without courage is a Sports car without fuel.

Natural leaders are an embodiment of many key elements of leadership. They posses hunger for knowledge, which delivers the clarity they need. Clarity creates conviction. Conviction triggers confidence and confidence allows attachment to strong values. Strong values drive courage to the surface...and we sigh..."what a leader!"

Knowledge > Clarity
Clarity > Conviction
Conviction > Confidence
Confidence > Strong Values
Strong Values > Courage

The journey of a natural leader will follow this path irrespective of their exposures and education because they pave their own roads.

CHAPTER 3: THE NATURAL LEARNER

That gives birth to Natural Leaders and vice versa

The Outlier

Does natural learning lead to the birth of a natural leader or does natural leadership result in a different style of learning? **This question requires many more years of study but what can be safely said is that there is no surprise, many natural leaders are outliers in several ways - they do learn differently.**

What you will see them dominantly displaying, is outstanding LEARNING AGILITY. So what is Learning agility or what are characteristic of a person with high learning agility?

1) They possess an inbuilt CPU that gathers data and processes things in a snap and then begin to shape it into a map with routes

2) Connect information to what they already know and have read

3) Memory is a weapon and tool that they exercise really well, dipping into memory on the spur of the moment testing themselves and keeping their library updated

4) Show a unique capacity to recollect matter that is relevant promptly because of how they CATALOGUE information

5) This linking and co-linking skill allows a natural learner to not just be an expert in a domain, platform, function or subject...but also be among the first to latch on to the key ideas in a discussion.

6) Their uber alert mind is like a policeman with a baton knuckle knocking every blip, gap, error or miss, recognizing everything that sits well or works in sync

7) What often amazes others is this leader's ability to be a master critique who is constructive as well, because as soon as they find holes they also can tell you how to fix it – mostly using common sense.

8) Natural learners show the inclination to grasp and fathom things outside of their educational qualification mainly driven by the sheer force of interest they have constantly carried within them.

This breaking of walls is what makes natural leaders intimidating. There is almost nothing that can keep them out.

Their unique journey towards self development

The insatiable quest for knowledge and the desire to learn never ebbs, regardless of their biological ageing. In fact the peculiarity of a natural leader is that as they age they become even hungrier; building a ravenous appetite for knowledge like they are conscious of time running out. **This is when the learner becomes a seeker. Seekers** try all avenues; take all kinds of roads to discover themselves first. Then they go on to seek the truth of human needs, motives and behavior while fathoming with equal aplomb how business functions and does not. What machinery in the eco system of work and life works well and how. What is the fuel that keeps things well oiled, the reason some people and business survive, how best to thrive and the order of patterns.

How they look at the SOURCE of learning

Natural learners gain wisdom from all and sundry; never discriminating the teacher nor the messiahs of a message. Those who revere only an education and learning which comes from a college over what life can teach will miss most such glorious texts. The trouble with these texts is that they are abstract. They are found by only those eyes and ears that are tuned to find them. The texts are not hard bound with a cover page, index, content, tests and references. The texts we talk of here are volatile, loosely occurring and require a very agile mind with heightened senses to be stitching them together to form an index with content and references. The cosmic library thus lies in the head of the natural learner who posesses the ability to synthesize and make sense of what is not so obvious. **This is why many natural learners are natural leaders too.**

Mastering the Senses

Natural learners have a tendency to not follow rule books at times. They don't use one sense at a time. For example: they listen to more than what is said in the moment, drawing inference from multiple on-the-spot referencing picked up by their other senses. When they see things, they are using more than just eyes. **Perceptiveness therefore is their strength. Over time natural learners learn to make accurate guesstimates and predict human behavior with precision.** This also makes them a good judge of people, sound pragmatic decision makers, very effective coaches and influencing managers. Extrapolating meaning from innocuous events happens seamlessly - without conscious effort. This can happen only if you have fine tuned your senses to communicate with each other. **The constant employment of senses as hound dogs means Natural learners don't miss out on things in the cacophonous humdrum of life.**

Philosophy of Everyday Life is a CLASSROOM

A regular life offers zillion avenues to grow, learn, shape up, change and with that evolve — the one who catches most of these free lessons is the natural learner.

"When you come from a place that believes there is no better teacher than the rising sun and the setting star and everything in between...the whole world is a classroom."

Between the waking hours from dawn to night, if one seeks to learn a new thing each day – we truly can add to the knowledge bank. The problem is most of us can't pause long enough to do that. Natural learners have mastered the art of calming down. The active mind needs shutters. Just sleep is NOT enough. If you need all your senses to be heightened and always stand by as slave — they need their rest too. A mind that operates at that level of maturity knows how to feed it and provide much needed rest it deserves to work at optimum. Some opt for relaxation methods that are regimented like meditation, yoga or exercise while some others get cathartic with cooking, gardening and other hobbies to divert the mind towards calmness. Like when you start disk cleaning, your system knows its cleaning and prompts appear asking you to shut down applications....likewise the practitioner of planned mind rest informs the brain and the mind of what the process will be and what to expect. Word directions to the mind get the mind to behave.

Living every moment FULLY

Lifestyles have transformed us to mechanically go on doing chores so we work and juggle till we are totally consumed. Technology has come as a helping robotic arm but we have willingly enslaved ourselves to its many lures as well. What came as aid has now made us its dependents. Natural Leaders practice SNAPPING. They free themselves from unwanted extra chores without guilt. They minimize commitments and delete demanding people from life too if they are okay to be eliminated. They reduce their involvement with social media sporadically. In many cases they are not TV addicts at all. Parties and social events see limited participation from them — only as much is needed to stay within the community and work circle. When all frills are loosened, Time rises from the pile of "unnecessaries" that had hidden it deep under. Natural learners have planned time tables to rewind and think about the day that was.

Introspection and retrospection are key to the Natural learner without which their precious observations will make no sense. These are the two wheels of observation… which is nowadays a dying ability. Like the ability for intuition waned in man out of disuse, observation power will also fade away the more we depend on technology to do all our thinking and processing. But natural learners struggle to keep this side of them chiseled despite all the distractions and excuses possible. They know at some spiritual level they live differently and what makes them different from others is the fact that they are the keenest observers in town. If only we all could focus on really living the moment fully; then each of us would end the day with many "I gutchings".

3.

Third Eye of a Leader & Observation

THIRD EYE OF A LEADER

The most critical and Key component of Leadership is being the Master OBSERVER

OBSERVATION - The seat of Power

Leadership, management and life skills are more allied than we think it is. One who is adept at one area, will find it easier to migrate their observation and application skills to other areas. The similarity in the three is owing to the fact that all areas pertain to how we think about things to direct our actions. When competencies are missing or not sharp, when leading ability suffers or critical life decisions go askew – where do you suppose the problem lies? In thinking.

The mind is the chairman that operates every aspect of our life. The trouble is many of us haven't really gotten to know this power house well. Those who do know the workings of their mind tend to do two things well.

1) Observe every leaf that flutters and the length of stillness in between each flutter too.

2) They find the time to assimilate what they have been "reading" to make sense of how they all tally or sit in.

Observation is the starting point of all successes. Anyone who tells you about people skills, business skills is still working on the icing of the cake. This is where substance lies and always will. **The best product of the best school can work with concepts and theories but if they can't detect all the variables, sense data, know their roles and continuously evolve they will still be a recipient of what is to happen; not be the designer of destiny.** One could have picked up socializing and networking skills but if they are not masterful in reading people, intent, motives both their professional and personal life will perennially see surprises and difficulties arising out of human relationships.

The Business space and the human domain – both solicit from us the same two items. OBSERVATION and time to PROCESS what is observed.

The existence of gut instinct is an enviable ability. We all know of people who have an uncanny ability to judge people accurately. They predict human actions and choices as well. In some ways they become soothsayers without being in the profession. The police, trained investigators, central intelligence, are trained to value observation and dedicatedly spend time in programming the mind to make sense of data all senses collect. People who do this without training to practice it each day make it a way of life. This is why they manage to protect their own interests and others, are able to forewarn of potential hazards and can predict who can be influenced and how.

Some who are exceptional masters of the two skills can also envision fiscal windfalls. There is math, logic, information and dependencies studied at lightning speed to be able to do that; but they manifest great comfort in being able to smoothly sail through. Stock brokers who invest for returns and agents who help organizations build treasury display this ability without which their role as sound consultants would not endure.

The political arena is not alien to the big two skills either. Politics is the oldest sparring arena of the mind. This does not refer to national or global politics alone. Politics exists in every strata and every square mile that is inhabited by human beings. A community of human settlers will urge the election of a leader and with leadership comes power and with power – politics. Allies, aides, conflicts, competition, enemies, opposition, games and ploys begin to surface. Where power is not attached to money, it is attached to position, recognition and name. Like in the case of religious centers, NGO's and community groups. The motivator is not always money. It could very well be an abstract place of reckoning which is coveted. The reactions of the mind however to attain that place is the same as someone who aspires for money and personal growth.

A company or an organization without an iota of politics is as possible as water without hydrogen will be. We need to understand that human society operates because of underlying agendas, intentions, energies and desires. Who is most vehement drives it and leads it while others follow. Who is the all seeing owl will know of what is happening and who is leading it is worth their time — is it's a cause they want to belong to at all. The eyes that see and the ears that hear everything will always be able to look out for themselves, not being a pawn in someone else's game. But to be able to do this seamlessly, being a devout observer is fundamental.

"The consciousness of mind and the mindfulness at all times is your Sword as much as it is you Shield."

The third eye of a Leader

Only the keen, dedicated observer has the third eye open. When you have two functional eyes with no malfunction in your optical system, you see what you see and process using the brain to make the most obvious connections. But this is normal sight. The opened third eye means a person has reached a place of complete control over the usage of the five senses including the sixth sense. Such a person is a voracious reader of people and events. The third eye sees everything that is outside the scope of the physical eye. The mind comes into play here, working up a synchronicity with the data senses are pulling up. Together they process information to understand everything in its individual setting and in co-relation. (It is important you don't mix this up with the opening of the Spiritual third eye that Hinduism teaches and shows how to master.)

Curiosity at the CORE

One whose third eye is working, will be like a precocious six year old with relentless curiosity. Curiosity is very important to comprehend here. One must remember that it is the initiator of energy. In a conditioned environment of a planned human society curiosity is permitted only in children. As we grow up, we are expected to toe-in-line and get predictable to be honorable citizens, teammates and members of the community. Such an existence that draws up a good list of what is okay and not, what can be done and not kills the sense of expedition and adventure in people. Most follow regimes from school to college to work to society till we get programmed into dropping curiosity. The**n transform into becoming conformists** because the rewards for agreeing are higher than questioning or exploring. People with the third eye open are NOT conformist. They manage the delicate balance of living in an adult society while nurturing their zealous curious child side.

The Signs

These are people who want to learn things even if that is not going to earn them bread. They ask scores of questions mainly to know and make sense of even the senseless things around them. Many of us look back and reminisce; but not always with the intent of reprocessing data to learn or find something new. For whom the third eye is open – this is a fixation and habit. They can look at what already happened over and over like professional investigators on a mission to find clues that lead to the murderer. Because what they experience is stored in permanent files they find it easy to ruminate, regurgitate it like lazy cows chewing on cud. But it is when the same events are thrown up over and over that a new finding hits them. A realization occurs or a fantastic trend is discovered.

While going through current events such observers create photographic memory, store key words people used, tones get registered and actions too are reeled into their film strip. This archived reel will get referred to later…leisurely in their own time…like a book they will read for themselves. When the third eye is open, people tend to show interest in very banal seeming things too. They watch everything however mundane it may appear because you never know what you will find and where. **The observer is the solver of all problems for self and others and they take that responsibility of vigilance seriously.** They are continuous learners who are growing each day wiser and better than yesterday in the hope they will be useful to the people and the work they do.

One who cannot read situations and people can be successful neither personally nor professionally. To manage others, we need to be able to manage self and before we develop others – be certain we are developing too.

This book thus is for the sharpening of the hardest skill there is – OBSERVATION, which is the mother of many competencies and skills. Be it Relationship building, Influencing, Strategy, Visioning, Negotiation, Persuasion, Building talent, Motivation, Decision Making, Communications or Inspiring others – just about everything will be impacted by the absence or presence of good observation skills. In a nutshell, Leadership and Management would be incomplete without observation. In fact, observation is the central nervous system to both. Yet it is the least talked about in academies and organizations perhaps because it is hard to teach. One requires sensitivity and strong five senses to get the sixth one working.

It is rare to find someone who will mentor us, direct our attention, present tests to guage our ability to soak life. Very few among us have real Life Coaches. Yet there are those who test their awareness and heightened senses, who test their personal journey in self development. For whom this journey has not yet begun, this book will help to check just how good an observer of life you are as of now and how far you could really go. If you are already a keen observer for whom learning from life has commenced; then the spiritual journey of meaning and depth is found in the simplest of situations. If so, then this book will resonate with your spirit urging you to augment your capabilities even further.

Source of the OBSERVATION Tests

Once we cover the journey of breaking bias, looking at learning and change differently we will embark on the part of the book that begins the jog – observation testing. This is the section where stories of people will be shared to test you ability to gather from it.

To bring opportunity to test observation, I have had to scrounge for some really simple yet thoughtful stories about real people I met. I prefer to bring to you cases that came from some of my travels and there is good reason for that. **Your third eye opens best when it is not bothered by the interference of duty, responsibilities and image to keep. We loosen our "controlled" spirit as we travel.**

"Travel becomes this thriving, esoteric abyss that offers so much for the Sindbad in you"

Every explorer has an undying Sindbad spirit which is why they are sagacious regardless of chronological or biological age. And this is when you begin to meet the most beautiful people out there who are life influencing. When a ticket to some place is in our hand, we somehow seem to break free from the shackles that bind us to the rigmarole of everyday schedule and routines. No better time to open the eye and watch the world. The best time to learn is thus when you travel.

I kept journals over the years on many subjects spanning life skills, relationships, workplace politics, leadership, psychology along with logs on my travels and what I learnt from each trip. After about three years of keeping these chronicles, I began listing entries as "My Travelearings". It became a concept that helped me draw out much from simple travels. Much learning I gained actually changed my philosophies, approach and perspectives forever.

Shared in this book are some of those compelling stories. Every story documented unique realizations. Over time they confirmed the possibility of learning from anywhere and anyone even while in-country. The archives became testimony to the fact that real wisdom and fresh outlook are reaped from areas outside the formal systems through experience; validating that simple regular people and events, are repositories of knowledge and learning even though our high handed urban thinking ends up valuing formal education the most.

What we need to know about life skills, leadership and self management can be picked up from our own Travel earnings. Hopefully by the end of this book you will begin to appreciate your own sojourns more; be an open student every time you hold a ticket to some place…also never let go of everyday lessons that are dished out while the hand of your watch moves to clock the passing of an hour or a day.

Gracias!

These stories are about seven people I met and they are the central characters from whom I learnt much and perhaps so will you. I have to start by thanking them for the chance meeting in life especially because tracing the first six is virtually impossible.

So who are these people?

I met them all during my travels in India, while on the job. As a traveler I have always enjoyed conversations that traversed lifestyle, choices, outlook, driving forces and the people in them. The cultural ways of a community, influences, how people understand life and it also prescribes a style to the people who live in it. I barely recall names of cities, hotels, restaurants or even the famous museums or shrines I have been to; however a person met and the tiniest details of all they shared – that I remember like it was yesterday. It is then that it occurred to me that much of my travel was more conversations with strangers than just looking around at sights and touristy destinations. The twist in my travel diaries is that it is not a barrage of historical places seen or about the 'must see' locations and the marvel in them – my travel journals were dedicated to the beauty I found in some very ordinary people met, who lived extraordinary lives. And while my happy-to-talk-to-strangers-tongue always elicits from others more than I bargained for – my hands have beavered most nights to register them in diaries which is what made it possible to pen this book so many years later.

The messengers

Travelers rarely ever meet the people they met again and I had been widely aware of that -which is what changed the nature of meetings. The people became precious; short visitors in life that you give the best of yourself to and from whom you expect nothing in return. And perhaps there sits the secret to great interactions.

The few that were truly extraordinaire' haunt my memories and I find it hard to believe these were just chance meetings. When wonderful people are met, they appear wonderful regardless of their abject poverty, simplicity or compounded issues.

To me it seems like divine consideration that allowed the crossing of our paths. **People come like messengers – they convey much, if we are willing to**

listen well. And if you are all out seeking them – then you will meet for sure. I profoundly thank all the mind liberating people I have met so far whose stories I have shared in the pages to come.

"To get to know a country, you must have direct contact with the earth. It's futile to gaze at the world through a car window." – Albert Einstein

4.

Stories and the Traveler

Why stories

To bring veracity to the claim that life is simple yet copious in its offering, I had to select the most straightforward and lucid medium of learning – stories. People's stories. Life offers opportunity equally to all of us.

"A rich life is one that allows meeting many people unlike you. And by that definition, someone poor is one who meets very few people in their life, mingles with only alike or stunts personal growth by interacting within socially acceptable circles."

Too much of your own society and neighborhood is not as much a limiter as not stepping out of four walls or being a recluse but it is certainly swimming in the same pond. When people are plentiful, the platter of exposure brings variety. It is impossible to boost personal growth by just being in a job, same house, with the same people and dutifully paying bills on time. The single-handed effort of training programs and academic curriculum directs you no doubt, but a holistic transformation requires us to learn from OTHER PEOPLE'S lives and messages.

An observation test could very well have been an intricate architecture of episodes designed like a murder mystery coaxing your conscious mind to fuse with your subconscious but it would not appeal to all. What appeals to all are stories about others. In that sense we have progressed, made technology our slave and we have in turn become slave to things that mechanically talk back to us...yet the magic of a story told is held up at a pristine altar still. Regardless of who we are in race, gender, faith or position – REAL stories of people never fail to absorb our mind. The tests ahead aims to absorb your mind firstly so that thinking is not a conscious process with heighted level of attention. You have to sail through this unaware that at the end of every story will come an opportunity to list out all that you discovered, realized, observed and take away to apply as a Life Skill, Management or Leadership parable.

When and if you decide to pick the top stories of your life to evaluate the college it has been for you...remember these encounters and chance meetings, don't demand long journeys with people. Transitory moments are good enough. Your own life's meeting of the Messiahs needs to be shared with family, friends and teams.

"Stories from life are an enriched personal treasury that gets heavier with every remembrance....a lighthouse we get to keep that will shine some light on dark nights as we struggle to navigate the angry seas of life"

Stories are ENERGY stirrers

I have been convinced of the power of storytelling. Most of my value orientation and interest in human behavior started when I was a child listening to the stories my aunts, mother or father narrated. Over time, I noticed that stories convince people faster, impress far more and last in the mind as well – long enough to bring change. Stories are very potent even at the workplace. Debates can be won by deploying the right story at the right time. Being a professional in the talent and HR space, I have used narratives to substantiate a poignant idea or value and it has always given agreeable results. They go far deeper than models/steps or frameworks. Man was not meant to be clinical, else emotions would have been deleted from our profile. Most failures in life occur when people think exclusively isolating feelings. We learn things as we grow academically and are required to demonstrate them but there is no better way to accept and incorporate principles, outlook and behavior than to believe in it. In my experience, the way belief comes naturally is through real stories.

When I observe people and events – I write as I see them without judging – then extrapolate the key elements, patterns and finds. That is how stories turn into curriculum and that is how you will need to start keeping notes if you wish to experiment likewise.

Strange thing about Stories and Schema

Stories of our life are locked up in several schemas. A schema in psychological terms is a cognitive framework or concept that helps organize and interpret information by grouping them. Each individual has several such schemas in the CPU of their mind. One that collects all related material attached to say paracetamol, bedbugs, karma, biking, horticulture, dating, aging so on and so forth. A schema can contain learnt formal concepts and some that you add in your repository basis your own life experiences, what you heard or saw and all that you have inferred from exposure.

It is like a box where a subject is segregated by headers and related branches set by relevance. A person dips into a schema when an opportunity demands sharing them. **People who are attached to stories usually have them right at the top of the box within easy reach, which is why they become powerful influencers, whose spoken words actually move people.** Some actually move on to harness this skill into a profession and become motivational speakers and transformationists.

Emotions create Visuals that last

Adults are hard to move by logic and ideas alone, because each of us have our own basket of it. People shift faster into being convinced and influenced when they were made to feel things. **Emotions are still what govern our assessments and agreements. When lucid visualizations begin in response to a story that is told...the listener has packed their bags and has already started travelling with you.** Audio always stimulates the creation of a video for the listener. There is no way we can listen to a story and keep imagination at bay.

Visualization makes things come alive. In that moment the story has moved from speaker to the listener, to keep or discard. And when a narrator is passionate, a listener can be lured to believing that it indeed was a time and place they both shared. **If the listener repeats that story a few times to others and masters that story – it truly becomes their story. One that they lived over many times in their head and felt strongly about, enough to repeat. That is how we own stories and through stories own, share and transfer REAL knowledge.**

What you ought to know

The best ways to enter another man's heart is not through the stomach – it is through the ears. Funnily, even as we read, we speak in our heads. Soft voices to ourselves and in doing so, we are the speaker and we are the listener too. Reading, thus, is a powerful medium; one that will not find competition in any movie regardless of the animation or action films brag of. The mind is a fabulous creative director, cinematographer and visual expert. THAT is the power of learning from stories. All these get kicked up at the same time to make a blockbuster. Your private cinema viewing experience in which you travel as far and as deep as you choose. However one must remember not all stories have great meaning, value or impact to be stashed away in a Schema. Stories that have explicit content, much meaning and passionate embrace of relevance makes it to the minds cellar. Once memory identifies a story as a collectible it will sit in the schema perhaps unopened for years but because good data is not lost; reappears decades later even surprising you sometimes, "How come I didn't forget this?"

"A narrative is to learning formats what the sun is to our solar system. It is the gravitational pull at the center that commands all."

Travel and FREE schooling

"My education was interrupted only by schooling. I began my education at a very early age in fact right after I left college." – Winston Churchill

Whoever knows the weight of the lines above are people who experiment and explore other ways to learn and grow. Such learning comes outside of orchestrated formal content testing the learner's ability to study, see, sense when there are no books, questions or reference guides. A person's natural intellect is thus sharpened. The environment turns into a catalyst. And that learning would have sat camouflaged in problems, in street fights, in arguments, in dissidence, in weird practices of a strange community, in eating strange foods, in making a friend from another race, in being part of a family that's not yours or even in learning to see God in a place your holy book does not prescribe it.

"The liberated mind is the only one fertile enough to allow new ideas to germinate."

A child whose family has to travel much is in touch with new lands and people. He/she will be quick to connect with strangers, make new friends, learn new skills, imbibe local sensitivities and sharp enough to fathom psychological makeup of people. As it is kids adapt the fastest but kids who have travelled much have a few more stars pinned on their lapels. They show cultural sensitization skills, readily give room to new ideas, respect differences, and change more readily than anyone who learnt change management in a corporate classroom! One of the best and richest source of abundant lessons thus is travel. And this is because the mind is most willing and yielding when set free from what binds it to rudimentary life. The qualifications of a traveler hold greater value than any regular endorsement. Travelers learn for life. They are the utilitarian pupils who learn from anything. The learning is original, it is deeply stirring, it is prolific and infectious...because it is conviction that comes from truly believing.

"A man travels the world over in search of what he needs and returns home to find it." – George Moore

I loved Paulo Coelho's The Alchemist for the simple reason that it highlights simplicity of existence. Somewhere early in the pages, I realized the search has to end at the feet and if it won't, I am rejecting this book and rubbishing the whole idea of having to search all over for what we seek. Well, we all know the master writer did a monumental job of writing pages after pages when he knew only the last few mattered. But the journey to that realization is equally important as the moment of awareness and his book did such justice, it is hard for my humble pen to offer him praise. He keeps the reader engaged and enthralled and then drops a bucket of water on the head. A cold awakening to a rude fact. All you need is right here right now – always was and will be.

It has become the in thing; rather classy to say "I travel to learn about the world, to seek greater knowledge". But that cannot come from holding cameras, sipping fruit drinks and following scenic paths. That kind of travel is for fun. There have been true seekers in history who travelled to meet people and study the place in context to culture, habits, science and values. **An education coming out of travel is not what can be easily captured in reels of film. It is stored in schema of the human mind that exerts pressure on the spirit and changes behavior bringing about an evolution that colleges aspire and parents perennially wish for their child.** All that you want to learn is in your home country. It will not require hundreds of stamps on twelve passports.

How Travel was seen in Historical times

Regency Period and muses

This attachment to mental stimulation by people different from me has something to do with books I read about old Europe. I have been addicted to books written in the Regency period for over two decades.

Many classics revealed the importance of human conversations in the period when television, internet and social media were non-existent, thereby throwing the human mind to seek other people for thought stimulation. Writers like Shelly, Oscar Wilde and Rudyard Kipling travelled much. They talked and met people across all strata to sink into the realities of mankind's ways, no matter where they came from and regardless of how unlike they were. They were either sparked by such catalysts or stirred to intellectualize. Anyway, they wove into their concepts and writings what they learned from such co-existence. **Learning from travel is not a new age wisdom thus. The best of thinkers and writers have sworn by it centuries ago. It's just that we have other distractions today that lessened the shine of the most promising one.**

Early Britain prepared for bad winters by sending out invitation to thinkers, writers, philosophers, poets, and musicians if they could afford to be host to an intelligent well-traveled mind in their homes. That ensured brightness through damp, dark days. The conservative yet seeking host could draw warmth from a traveler's sermon although most such hosts didn't go around much themselves. The seventeenth to nineteenth century was rich in this concept of positive entertainment. Who could not think differently or grow outside of books – would seek a traveler to spar with, debate, think with and reinvent self in the comfort of their own four walls. I personally love this period which accepted a traveler as the most evolved in the hierarchy of people because they are who dared to set foot across lands.

Almost all writers in good health beat the wicked season of cold and dampness by travelling to countries that tickled their interest and that is when their pen got mighty. **European travelers from the bygone ages, lived in strange places for months and at times stayed on for years only to shake their own presumptions and to gain new ideas that conceptualized contemporary ideas worthy of taking pen to paper.** They stirred the community and created renaissance by the ability to keep the mind vitalized.

Depression and melancholy was common in countries where the weather was unkind. Physicians of the period advised travelling to stir the mind. Most ailments are psychological was the premise and it is indeed amazing that many cured themselves without dependent drugs...only by the power of a new land. Fresh places hold the magic trident.

1) Calm coming from being away from all you know

2) Hope from realizing there are places where nothing is tainted by memory and holds mysteries

3) Positivity that comes from better health of mind and body which eventually permits better human connections and experiences

We have forgotten that travel is an alternative to medication and is an alternative for education as well.

Why are the Stories from India?

I picked stories and events from India for a good reason. Being Indian if I were to base tests on people and events from outside India who I met during travels, it would suggest to some readers that one needs to traverse other geographies to amass their own repository of learning which would be utterly wrong. All you need and seek is in your home country…provided you respect the roads.

My job and projects opened gates to much travel. I met some outstanding people and had stupendous realizations from watching, listening or talking to folks from all over. I have consciously picked those memoirs that were poignant for me. They come from various states of India; predominantly from the north, west and south of India. East India is my dream destination and await opportunity to catalog stories from there soon.

Your lessons can be within miles of you, in another city nearby, down four blocks or right in the neighborhood. What happens with most of us is something fascinatingly common – we are more controlled and restrictive of ourselves in known environments. There are people who go through very tough phases in life but don't have the time to pause, introspect and think through because each day demands forty-eight hours out of them. Others need not have a pressing life phase but the lull of existence and routines stunts the mind. Life drills make one lose the ability to be a soaking sponge.

We grow bolder, more liberal and persuasive when we are away from roads, signboards and familiar faces. It is almost like a new place allows you more room to be yourself or be someone else whichever be the case. Regardless – If you seek teachers in people, you will find. The world is a repository of lessons and wisdom galore in equal measures. There is not one geography prescribed by an atlas that promises higher evolution. Your homeland, wherever that may be holds the promise for all that you will ever need. That fairness, is the beauty a mature traveler heart of heart always knows....and cherishes. India is my country and stories thus are from the length and breath of my beautiful homeland.

The Vacationer, the Tourist and the Traveler

There are different types of travels and it depends on the mental makeup of the voyager.

A vacationer: is one who plans a travel to get that much needed break. To unwind. To relax. Spend time with family. To share space and time in another land alone or with those they love. To show children a new country. To give the spouse a dedicated few uninterrupted days. Vacationers come to see, to smell, to taste, to disconnect and feel something else – to be anew. That is a different need – one connected to work life balance and stress management. And a good one too. So who is a tourist and who is the traveler?

A tourist: Travel entails

- Selection based on reputation (its popularity)
- Or even how uncommon it is – Discovery of a new destination
- Promising views and sights
- Culinary offering and events
- Societal pressure. Like when a certain society circle claims it is "in" to travel to XYZ; it becomes a must do. More so if it is expensive, exclusive or exhilarating
- Hotels, places and restaurants are most important and to be memorized as well
- Having a planned schedule and timetable
- A tourist comes to strike off a country on their list of places to go to before they die. It is a bucket list journey. One that is not profound but fast paced to actually tick mark as many places as can be before the Visa for life expires. Hurriedly going through an agenda based calendar, cannot offer much learning. Amidst this mayhem, there could be a splattering of good things heard, read or people met but a tourist memorize places and foods, lanes and locales more because the trigger is more a need arising from vanity than naked curiosity. One big motivator for the tourist is to establish a reputation of seeing places – been there done that.

Who is a traveler then?

- A traveler has no agenda to satisfy a specific need
- They come with an open mind and have open days on calendar
- Any trip or distant travel, even work travel will convert itself into an opportunity
- They may be extroverted or introverted but on travels – they reach out
- They study a place in relation to the people and cultural practices not just sights, smells, shopping and taste
- They yearn to create memories by remembering people and CONVERSATIONS
- Are open to learn from other people's wisdom and insights

- They don't assess people by class, status or religion. A traveler sees people as seamless threads in the fabric of one human quilt
- They develop a persona that invites the speaker and sharer so others "find" them
- They listen deep enough to read between the lines and connect dots valuing a trip mainly because something priceless was realized or discovered in the mind while the feet covered distance

"The tourist pompously tells the world they are a traveler, while the traveler doesn't care a dime what they are called except who calls out to them."

7 Stories to gauge your Sensitivity, Consciousness and Observation Power

Story 1
Resilience fights all Tides
On Energy, Fighting spirit and Pride

I met a poor gardener on the outskirts of Hyderabad. His story is unique because his philosophy far surpassed his education or his exposure in life. Like words from an old soul that reverberate in the mind because all of it made sense. His relentless spirit is what human strength is made of. For everyone who is tired and exasperated with life – here is something that will make you want to wake up and take charge!

I was going to Hyderabad for work that summer, and it was a blazing hot that year. We were right in the middle of May, which pretty well describes an Indian summer in all its wrath. It was burning; humid and agonizing in Mumbai, but Hyderabad would be far hotter everyone warned me. I researched on what places I ought to see while I am there – provided there was enough life left in me to pick myself up after dripping pails of perspiration. Shopping and few historical sites came up on search engines but how much could you do in scorching heat that would be around forty-four degrees? It's hardly comfortable going about doing touristy things while being caked in anti sun tan SPF 70.

I had traveled to this city before but that was such a fleeting trip, I didn't have the time to schedule anything worthy of my interest; so this time, I was hell bent to make it memorable. That's when I found a strange something on Google – so many old age homes in and about the city; and there was one in particular that has many pictures. Someone at work too had mentioned it. This place was giving a fresh leash of life to many old folks whose children had cast them off for being old and incapacitated. Obviously many of these disposed old folks were parents to some uncaring children going through much emotional trauma. I read then about some old age homes and the stories of their inmates. Some had worked hard and sent children off to study to acquire a good education, pledging their only home and farms, to see their children leave them with huge mortgages and no support. Most kids never returned or helped the parents. While in a country like India abandoning aged parents is not the culture. it is not entirely unheard of either. Perhaps we baulk at it more because of how our society looks at this primary duty - a Karma one cannot ignore.

Such abandoned old couples found the communities they lived in would help them out till they could and then finally when money hits rock bottom a bank they owe to would show up and liquidate their property, leaving two old people on the street. There was an old age home in Mumbai I had wanted to visit but the city being as congested as it is, traveling was a nightmare. Visiting an old age home outside in another less populated city with less traffic made sense and this trip looked like it would be the one.

There was one particular old age home I wanted to go to on one of the afternoons, when I got off work early. I had started work early that morning when I had planned to make the visit so I could leave office early as well. I told a colleague that I wanted to go see a particular old age home that had earned a good name. "There are so many old age homes here close to Hyderabad, why?" I asked her. She laughed at my peculiar interest because I was apparently the first colleague from Mumbai who was not asking to go see the pearl and silk market that Hyderabad was famous for. She told me from what she had heard the old people come from several small districts around Hyderabad. To her young mind, I was being preposterous; wasting my time studying something while there were better things to mull over.

Word spread in that small office of how I was going to study old people and their psychology. The jabs and jokes went all day and it became clear nobody would accompany me; that I would have to march out there myself. I called for a cab and was waiting at a restaurant in a hotel that was supposedly a landmark. The cabbie claimed to be on his way. It looked like another fifteen minutes of waiting. I plonked on an iron garden chair which had a wide canopy umbrella, keeping the almost scalding sun away while also letting some breeze come my way. I looked around for a newspaper so I could fan myself. The wind was being stingy and the barely working ceiling fan was painstakingly slow. That's when my eyes fell on an old gardener who was pulling weeds from the lawn right next to my table. He was too old to be sitting on his haunches weeding and snipping grass with giant hand-held iron blades. I was afraid he would topple over and never get up again.

So I walked over to the tiny fence that separated the open café from the garden. From here I could see him better.There was an outdoor fan there that worked up a storm of breeze and it was like a magnet in such unkind weather. The tall pedestal fan began blowing wind in my hair and I suddenly felt like a model from those shampoo commercials, swaying tresses all over. Only, in my case there just was no sophistication at all – I was troubled, pulling hair out of my mouth, eyes, and pushing them behind my ear all the time. He looked up many times and each time there was me trying hard to handle my own hair. This went on half a dozen times. Then he smiled at me, stood up and walked over. He must have been between seventy-eight to eighty-two. Somewhere there- Too many wrinkles to tell his age.

He was bent in the spine a bit and wobbled sideways as he walked. Wore the local checkered lungi, which is a large cloth men wear at the waist that can be folded into half as they sit or work. He picked up the mighty fan and turned it in another direction and suddenly I was aware of his strength even at that age. He said he saved a goddess today, so it must be his lucky day. Of course I too laughed at the idea of a hapless, confused goddess who couldn't even help control the hair on her head, let alone help anyone else. He nodded and walked back to his grass and I had this urge to talk to him. In him there was a story – breaking to make its opening and I had to find the guts to overcome my inhibitions. The cab driver called again. He said he had a flat tyre and was working on it. It would take an hour now but long distance travel required booked cabs only, so it was apparent I had enough time to kill. I looked at the old gardener with new found determination. Politely I asked him his name to which he replied "Nagappa". He shyly asked me who I was. I gave him a boring introduction to myself and as I was telling him what I do, I suddenly realized how utterly 'lack luster' I sounded. They are a standard set of four lines that constitute my introduction. It carries my name, city of origin, and what I do for a living, and I usually closed with what brought me to the host city. I can translate these four lines into at least four languages with ease which is the only variation. I shut my mouth. It dawned on me that he had said one word, "Nagappa", and I gave him four lines. I have to learn to talk less!

He nodded like he couldn't care how many words I was using though. For a bit, I thought I was capable of boring even an old man. Obviously he had no interest in conversing with a woman of my age or profile. Either that or he was being professional. I was fumbling in my mind on what to say, when he suddenly broke the glacier that had formed between us. "I had a girl like you. She is about your age now, give or take two to three years. I have two boys as well. When I saw you, I couldn't help think about her. She has your eyes, big and black. She was always tactless like you – dropping things and falling as well." Feedback already? I scanned my memory, where did he get that from? I was the real world Alley Mc Beal but someone has to watch me for a while to know that. Oh! So he had seen me stumble up the small stairs on the way when I almost dropped my laptop bag. "Since when has he been watching me?" I wondered.

I expressed how my sixth sense has picked up the existence of a poignant story sitting in him. Perhaps not in his present; but his past. He nodded, his small, beady eyes looking right at me. Nagappa scrapped some clay from his sickle and looked like he was reminiscing. Then he sat down on the grass with his long thin legs stretching out. It looked creepy for a moment. Legs that thin with knee joints jutting outwards — I had not seen anything like that. He shifted. Sat on his haunches again drawing his knees all the way up to his chin. How can someone do that! So lithe so nimble so effortless. That is what poverty does…it builds amazing zero fat bodies that are sturdy even when old. Then it struck me, village folks across Indian sit on their haunches seventy per cent of the day and are super flexible; have no fat on the belly and are totally capable of drawing the knees to reach their chest comfortably to even rest their chin on it if they wanted to. Belly fat is the first killer of fitness. Nagappa was getting comfy to tell me a long story, I could tell. He pulled out a beedi (tobacco wound in leaf) and began smoking; a sign he was about to narrate something and the beedi will expedite his ability to remember. I too pulled my chair closer and got ready to hear this blast from the past. **People always pick up their favorite habits when they begin to talk – especially when they want to open up. It is a proven natural recourse – like it brings immense comfort to the speaker and helps them unwind before they get wound up in their own story.**

Almost sixty years ago, Nagappa had left his hometown to seek his fortune. It was important for a young lad to leave the village if he wanted a better life. For village folk this idea is always based on the fact that new surroundings offer fresh opportunities. Jobs that they would not take in their home town – they are willing to take elsewhere. There is no shame in labor, in working hard and doing anything it takes when people don't know you. That's how the poor work their way up. Go to a city where nobody knows them; abandon pride and self image, take up any random job available- save - seek better opportunities and send money home. A new city presents new learning, new chances, new gurus, new perspectives and a new destiny. **It is amazing how the poor see possibility by just changing the scene while the comfortable have to be 'taught' to step out of the comfort zone in workshops and programs.** I knew Nagappa was going to drop pearls of wisdom every step of the way.

Many decades ago Nagappa had caught a train and landed in Mumbai where he worked odd jobs at first. He later found apprenticeship under a mason and accepted the terribly long working hours in exchange for an opportunity at learning new skills. This was going to teach him much. So he worked fourteen to sixteen hours every day for five years till he mastered all there was to learn as a mason. One day, he decided he needs to move out of this city if he had to grow. Here he was known as a laborer who was working under a well established mason. He didn't want to compete against his master and fight for the same customers. There was a need to start on his own, so fresh territory had to be sought. He caught a train and came to Bangalore. The city was beautiful in those days. Green, clean, organized. Bungalows were everywhere. Thousands of independent houses were cropping up everywhere. He started taking up contracts for masonry and hired a few people for work. Business was doing well and he began making the money he always dreamed of. He visited his village after nine years — now a successful man. His old mother was so worried for him that she got him married on that same trip. Within five years, Nagappa was father to a pair of twin boys and a girl. There many more mouths to feed but he was doing well for himself.

He had earned a prestigious project that was going to build a gated community of bungalows. He had won the masonry contract for over two dozen houses there. The project was a huge success. A wealthy man who owned a house there later approached him to lead another project. This was on an expensive farm house he was building next. Nagappa was very hopeful this will provide him the credibility needed to also do artistic work and not just functional masonry. Unfortunately, the project began showing money crunch in within months. The man who was developing this grand farm house slowly began avoiding him. He sensed trouble. Most of Nagappa's business was managed on credit and payments suffer when funds don't come on time from a client. But he badly wanted this project to declare his success. His reputation and future business was at stake. The six thousand square feet house was being built on a twenty-five thousand square feet property and it was going to be the brightest and biggest singular project Nagappa had been a contractor for. He didn't call the client or hound him sending umpteen messages; instead he decided to meet the owner in person at his office.

Nagappa had gone an angry, worried man but what happened at that meeting completely changed the way he thought about his client. Nagappa had built his arguments and his defense lines and his demand list to the T. When he appeared there; he was given audience without any drama. The man who was avoiding him was sitting across the table looking gaunt. Nagappa looked at the man's face and decided in the spur of the moment he needs to start with knowing what is the problem here – not his demands or dues. The genuine enquiry opened up a honest conversation between the two - the kind two honest people can have. The client appeared to be a reasonable gentle man who was intentionally right – just badly placed in time.

They both talked openly of their individual predicaments. No yelling, no screaming, and no threats. But as he listened to the man speak Nagappa realized the other man was far worse off than him. **We always think our own situations are the worst. 'The boil on my back will always be worse than your missing leg.'** There stood in front in front of him a man who could lose this house he was building and possibly have to sell the one he lives in as well to cover for losses made in business. If he couldn't raise money to fund his business now, he was finished. His partner had run away siphoning company money and was untraceable. Now he was left to answer people and pay for it himself before courts give verdict. The more Nagappa thought he became clear – he could always find another lucrative project and extend credits till he cleared dues. He had options and he has more business around the corner – this man has nowhere to go. His own situation was not as grave as the one this man was facing.

He came back home solemn…thinking about that other man more than he did about himself. His client had saved for several years to build this dream house. Just weeks before his loan from the bank came through is when he found out his partner had siphoned off large sums and created debts that he was not aware of. Nagappa thought hard. He had an idea...if it worked out this would breathe new life into the project and save everyone. He knew Sheikh, a man he had worked for before, on another development project. Sheikh was an established automobile dealer. Nagappa made him the offer of funding the rest of the property's development cost to take a partnership percentage in the sale that would come of it. That way Sheikh would fund the remaining thirty per cent of the project and take thirty per cent during its sale. If the bank attached the property, his client would be at a big loss. If this worked – there would be three happy parties at the end of it. Sheikh saw profit here and Nagappas client was marveled at the idea. Everyone agreed. They made it happen! This episode was a game changer in Nagappa's life. People revered him. He was known as a business man with a heart. Work came to him without having to chase after it. Feeding his family was easy there on.

Nagappa put his kids through the best of schools and colleges. The kids were academically very strong. They excelled in whatever fields they chose. As a father, he was never short on anything to give or do. His daughter was married off to an IT engineer in the United States. One son worked as a civil engineer in Delhi on some government projects, the other son was an eye specialist. He funded their ambitions to study further and acquire business management degrees and doctorates as well. Then his luck ran out. Some investments he had made in land crashed badly. He was getting older and admitted to having lost his touch. But his kids would not help out. It was below their dignity and education to be party to work that entailed dealing with labourers and workers. His wife developed a debilitating disease. Understanding the peculiar Hindi spoken in this part of India was hard for me, but from what he said it sounded like Alzheimer's. He shut his shop, tended to his wife he loved so much and nursed her, cooked, fed her and did all he could. The daughter ran into some monetary issues and sought the father's help. He couldn't say no to his only girl and so he pledged his only house. She had promised to pay back but never returned it. He pleaded his sons who now work and earn well to help but none came forth. They said it was his foolhardiness to trust his son-in-law, so he ought to pay the price of blindness himself.

In time the bank liquidated his house. The children refused to host the two aged parents so he moved in with his brother. Nagappa looked at the trees far beyond, "Nobody treats anyone with kindness when they are penniless. Your sense of duty and your good karma feeds your soul. But to expect others to remember your deeds and choices to repay acts of kindness later is foolishness. We all do what we think is right for us. My children are doing what they think is right for them. Likewise, I had to do what is right for me…to survive". Nagappa had to finally move into an old age home when his brother's hospitality ceased. But a man who had lived a life of independence, of social belonging, of good reputation, found it hard to be an invalid who will be cared for till death arrived. His wife needed medical attention and he just could not manage that alone.

Another old man at the old age home had a son who visited him at least once a month. That good friend helped Nagappa get this job here as a gardener. It gives him a room to live in, a small garden of his own behind the room where he grows vegetables, free food, no bills really and for as long as he can stand vertical and come to work, Nagappa said he will. Nagappa goes to meet his wife every other day but her memory is weak and she is not doing well.

But he won't give up working, he said. He knows nothing else besides being gainful. The only time he let work aside was when his wife was ill. **Empty mind will go to complete ruin if it has no purpose he said. Spirit is lost when it is not employed and it is our duty to give it a job – stay applied. Body is the first to be attacked by an idle mind. It will either bloat or go weak and get susceptible to disease or the inactive body begins to eat your spirit**. Then he laughed. "I have no money to be able to afford the luxury of getting sick and then treating myself. When I get sick, that will be the end of me. I am not afraid to die."

"Nagappa is a self-made man. With or without his children, he has always fended and provided for himself. If this is all I can do today for bread and butter; if this is my lifestyle — then so be it. My poverty is the price I have to pay for my folly and gullibility. No point blaming anyone or destiny either." In his words I heard pride standing tall still. To my unbiased eyes towards the end of his life, Nagappa has gone back to being that village boy who left home…without regrets, comfortable in his skin despite the beads of sweat on his forehead. He looked at life as an outcome of his actions and was willing to accept all its results whether good or bad. No cursing, no blaming, finding his peace in a clam existence.

The cab honked for me. I excused myself, went over to tell the cabbie that I don't need to go to the old age home anymore. I paid him for coming over. Then went back to Nagappa and told him – "Someday, Nagappa, I will write about you. About your grit and your pride. How you lived an extraordinary life of duty, values and character that many find hard to emulate. That in him was the greatest example of resilience, Fortitude of Pride, Composure and Forgiveness too." So saying I bid him goodbye. From the corner of my eye I could tell he was watching me go just as he had watched me come in.

He reminded me of one more something and I could not place what it was. While I was returning and was on the plane – it hit me. Before take off, the voice went, "In the event of an emergency water landing – please fix the oxygen mask to yourself before you help others." Nagappa was like that voice and message. Infact he lived up to that message all the way. No matter who you love and how much – take care of yourself. Nobody cares once all the care from you is extracted, and you are worth nothing. The abundant old age homes of Hyderabad will stand testimony to this realization. It is the country's second largest city with abused and aged who are abandoned by well to do children. The IT and education boom brought qualifications and employment to cities and towns around. But somewhere the beneficiaries of positive change forgot those who got them there. Bangalore and Hyderabad are India's capitals for aged rejects. When the nouveau rich settle down and come back to senses, we hope India won't require old age homes. Either that or people better learn from Nagappa - prepare for rainy days because when it rains; it won't stop just because you are old.

My notes: On Life skills / Management and Leadership

If you've run out of space – You are Gutching!

Nagappa didn't say but said anyway

1. One has to leave what is known and familiar to make fresh beginnings. If the current does not bring the desired outcome – move away. While it will be hard to pluck oneself out of there and find the courage to plant yourself elsewhere…it must be done.

2. When you plant yourself in a new place, it will not be an easy road. Sense of entitlement will not take you far. Humility is a MUST at the start of a career. One needs willingness to be malleable and ductile; to be bent and twisted in high pressure to be ready for new learning and fresh skills.

3. Be open to new opportunities even if they don't look fancy. Experience is what counts. One who won't count the hours is the one who will master soonest.

4. Respect for your teacher, your guru is another way of showing character. One who learns and then bites the master won't go far. Best to go far and then be all that you have to be…you are sure to flower that way.

5. Ethics are indeed a matter of choice but every time you make the hard but right decision – remember you are becoming a finer person. A fancy course or program cannot shape you into being a better human being. That kind of evolution can only come from thinking finer, doing better and choosing wiser.

6. Ambition fuels new ideas. Man without ambition is like a balloon with a hole, whatever air you fill in, will find its way out and that balloon will stay at either a constant or burst in exhaustion. Ambition is what triggers new thinking and dares one to take new roads, accepting paradigm shifts and displacement too.

7. We tend to view our misfortunes as the hardest and they appear to be grappling until we know what bothers the other. In some cases they are as innocent as we may be and our judgment of them could be unwarranted. We assume the worst of people. And most of that assumption is based on the façade of things we see. Every challenging situation needs less assumption and more of conversation/ investigation.

8. There is always a solution if you allow your mind to be a true problem solver. People attached to blame game extend issues rather than solve them. A person with a wherewithal to think is one who is less attached to personal gains only. One who is attached to selfish motives cannot think of win-wins. One cannot bring solutions that benefit the majority. They cannot be leaders. Someone who is stimulated by challenge can seek solutions antiseptically. Their results thus are best for all. This is how reputation is built.

9. Being dutiful and fair brings the joy of knowing one is right. Regardless of gratitude or returns from others; when we excel as people and professionals the

one thing that stays is self respect and virtue.

10. We must know our priorities in life always. A virtuous person needs no guidance to know that the balance of life at times will tilt and they willingly change focus because it is the need of the hour. Work-life balance is something everyone talks of but there will come times when one or the other – or both will be disturbed. If you ever need to make a conscious choice to sever from one to tend to the other (like Nagappa did to turn care giver to his wife) there can't and shouldn't be regrets.

11. To give, help, support beyond a point is folly. As a leader, manager or even parent, it is important to teach, show how things are done, be a good example, inculcate values and encourage education. But once they are ready and mature to apply their learning direction and guidance when they ask is all one needs to provide. To roll up sleeves, do their job or take on the burden of their duties is destroying their right to experience and fight wars using their skill. Bailing your team or your adult children only makes them weaker. There is a time for delegation and empowerment. Once you get there your role is by the stands where you watch them do their best. Allow them their mistakes. That is how they will grow. A sound leader, a strong parent knows when to say NO. They know when to ask subordinates/children to stand up on their own, just as they did. Being too permeable is mollycoddling. That is a disservice to their development and growth as adults and professionals.

12. Follow your heart and stay true to your spirit. Don't let the world's norms guide how you ought to think feel or act. Like Nagappa at the old age home — If situations are compelling a change – change. As long as you are willing to risk losing the security of what is known – go for it. At least you will find yourself in a place you walked into willingly and will also stay there by choice.

13. Be adaptive. Good days don't last forever. Success at profession does not indicate success always, nor does it mean happiness in the personal space is eternal. Life is about cycles. Business too has cycles. We all are happy to ride the tide when things are going great but a real warrior is one who shows equal stamina to fight the downtime and its odds.

14. Keep good cheer regardless of what time you face in life. Good people and good conversations are life's biggest treasure. Sad sacks and unhappy faces will barely ever draw anyone's curiosity. We live enriched lives when we share and gain from others.

15. Dignity is man's ability to rise high in career and social status with humility still attached. The job is NOT important – Dignity of labor is all that

matters. If time turns away its pretty face; then show that same grace you did in happier days. Do whatever you can to feed, fend and still stand up. Living on humble earnings is not the same as living on charity.

16. We make the mistake of calculating financial success by what we own, we drive and our standard of living today. Fiscal success in the materialist sense is ideally to be measured by what you planned to set aside that will assure a safe retrial. If a retirement plan can guarantee the lifestyle you have today, then you are home in calling it SAFE and today successful.

(Did you get all 16? Less or More?)

Story -2
Character is innate

On being a Change agent, BREAKING BIAS, on Pragmatism, Ownership and GUTS

This story is about the brave surrogate mothers in India who help infertile couples have children – who bring smiles to many homes, who have matured in human emotions to be consciously separate from the child they carry. Who help their own homes burn a better light that changes economics and the prospects of their own progeny. Most importantly, it is about biases we live with; the hold of society over minds and lives and what it takes to break from such shackles to lead others.

I was thirty-two and as naïve as they could possibly come at that age. I thought two people fall in love, marry, have babies, fight, grin and bear, forgive, support learn to smile, raise children and that is supposed to be family life. Many couples in India have a pattern that could have a different beginning because they didn't meet or fall in love with each other, but the progress after marriage is the same. Couples could get married through an arranged system where they don't necessarily know each other well. Families choose a groom or a bride based on background, education, prospects, similarity of culture etc as evaluators. From the day of marriage, the two strangers set foot into family life just like all those who marry the ones they love. In this case, it is learning to love who they are already married to. Both types have children, struggle to fend and feed if poor, hold responsibilities, and experience parenting woes plus its joys. In that sense - the journey begins to mirror each other regardless of how it started.

The idea that a family could be anything other than these two types never occurred to me. I was heading India West region Talent and OD at the time when

I was introduced to the type of family quite by chance. I had a lot of domestic travel on the cards those days. My daughters were in a boarding school and staying home drove me crazy so I was happy to be on the road. Traveling on the job kept my sanity by keeping the mind engaged. A house that is used to children is empty no matter how loud you play the TV or how much you try to sleep off the waking hours.

I would plan trips such that I would travel out Sunday and start work early morning on Monday. Likewise when activities were planned for later part of the week, I would make it spill over to Saturday so that is one day less of moping around between four walls. A trip was going to take me to Anand; a small city in Gujarat that carries a rather town like look and feel. This place is known for the White revolution (milk production) which was championed by Tribhuvandas Krishibhai Patel, a well known Freedom Fighter and Dr. Kurien. Their project metamorphosed the economic condition and also the communities here. People who languished in abject poverty moved on to being India's largest organized diary producing organization. They created history and became an object of many formal research studies.

Soon, almost every villager's home owned cows and they were educated on how to manage loans, feed, tend and procure more milk out of the cows. The diary plant purchased the milk from the villages and distributed the packaged milk and milk products. So when I heard I was to go to Anand, I was again reading, studying the economic reforms, statistic of women in dairy business, the legislatives and progress the banks and cooperatives there made.

Totally impressed, I landed in Anand on a Sunday. As I was driving to the hotel I noticed an IVF centre. Barely three hundred feet away another one that said sterility center, a little away further in a lane; three shops had been converted into a hospital that boasted of the best procedures in "Test Tube baby", a term many Indians still use to suggest medically aided reproduction. I raised an eyebrow. This is strange. I knew about the cows and the dairy business but what is this? It can't be that this entire place has reproduction issues? For a moment, I thought all that I read about the partial demise of mankind in the future by failure to reproduce and the inabilty to transfer Y-chromosome is indeed coming true - it is already happening here!

I had to find out what was happening in Anand. I checked into the hotel and decided I will walk around a bit. There was small salon for women on the same street. This wasn't the kind of place we see in cities. It looked more like an extension of someone's house. But I wasn't going to be too picky here. In the salon were some local beauticians and masseuse. Seeing a city-bred woman walk in, they began offering the most expensive of their treatments. Politely, I told them I was only looking for a relaxing foot massage, having been on the road non-stop for twenty days.

I plonked on a hokey pokey seat and a young woman began applying sweet smelling oil to my under feet. She wasn't so bad. She knew all the nerve points that a foot massage should cover at a pricey salon in Mumbai but then again reflexology and concepts such as these are east born. India and China were leaders of knowing and working on the human body long before English as a language decided to give such ancient knowledge English terms I mused. Villagers are natural experts of the massage space in India. Wrestling, village freestyle boxing, local martial art forms – all demand massages. This is the land of Ayurveda that emphasizes on better blood circulation for prevention of disease and also its cure. Most women of the village therefore know how to massage far better than city professionals who have to take up professional courses. While my train of thoughts ran on the subject I was feeling relaxed within five minutes of the process. There were no other customer around, so this won't be a hurried service and I could ask as many questions as I wanted- uninterrupted. Before luck ran out I had to collect all the information I could gather. So I made a passing remark about the innumerable IVF, sterility clinics lining roads and by-lanes. My masseuse looked up asked me if this was my first time in Anand. I told her it was.

She shrugged and said in a manner of matter of fact that some women lend their womb here for money, like she was telling me about an ice cream parlor selling vanilla and strawberry! I baulked and sat up in disbelief, yanking my foot from her hands a bit. She pulled my foot back and sternly looked at me suggesting my drama was tad too much. The women of Anand who volunteer to carry another couple's child for nine months peacefully hand over the baby when it's born, she said. I had heard of the concept of surrogacy, but back in 2008 it wasn't something we heard much of in India. I had not seen sterility clinics mushroom anywhere as much as they had in this town.

Greedy to know more, I asked her if she knew anyone who had been a surrogate mother. "Of course!" she replied! Turns out all four women in that small salon knew some woman or the other. I learnt the law and legislatives in the country were not mature at the time (Please remember that this is a story set in 2008 – the law today is fairly well defined on surrogacy. Much communication has happened on the process and entitlements through campaigns).

I was told the women and medical professionals who run these centers were rigorous in approach and discipline. They provide the best medical care and attention to the impregnated woman. They also ensure that the mother does not get attached to the baby and to make sure the woman is emotionally detached, they counsel her during the entire length of gestation. The surrogate mother usually does not meet the parents of the baby she will carry. At times however, some hopeful parents insist on meeting before the procedure begins. In some cases the meeting happens after the birth of the baby- during handover, to bring closure to the agreement. Some parents insist on the baby being breastfed for a month or so. Some happy parents stay in the city for a while and after thirty days take the baby away to begin their new life as family. The surrogate mother goes back to being mother to her own children and now with the money she earned for lending her womb, starts a small business, buys cows, or sets up a shop which is what most of them do with the money. The enterprising women of Anand had snapped away prejudice and bias attached to artificial insemination or carrying another's child to full term in a way most city-bred women like me could not.

I was desperate to meet one such woman in person. I asked them if they could introduce me to someone who had been a surrogate mother so I can understand the psychology, motivators and beliefs the surrogate mothers hold. I wanted to know what was the code of conduct these women followed in the society they live in. There was a lady in the salon who had been quiet all this while; she spoke from behind the cash counter. Her sister-in-law had been a surrogate mother and she could help me meet her if I was willing to go with her when she left work that day. I jumped at the prospect and now that it was settled, we chatted for the rest of the while the uncertified yet 'best in class' reflexology went on. What I had been listening to so far was only hear say; soon I was going to hear it first-hand.

The salon women had heard stories of surrogate mothers being sent great food, nutrition supplements, fruits etc from rich couples. One of them had heard of a woman who sobbed for months after handing over the baby. Some women had wanted to be surrogate again in a few years but medical experts do not permit repeat surrogacy apparently…at least not in a place where the options were several. I never managed to meet a doctor from there to confirm anything these women were talking about but with the time I had on hand I was lucky if I could at least meet a real surrogate mother.

Who I did get to meet was Jinalben. The lady behind the counter raised her voice to tell me Jinalben was coming over to the salon and I won't have to meet her in the evening. I was surprised at how interesting my evening was turning out to be. Half an hour later, a bell outside the salon rang. Jinalben came in, unsure and a tad awkward. She was a slim in frame, fair, sharp featured, not more than twenty-six, I thought. The lady in the salon told her why I wanted to meet her. But she only spoke the local Gujarati language fluently – her Hindi (language spoken with ease by many across India) was poor and I knew not a word of Gujarati except for kem cho (How do you do?). So I offered her my only two Gujarati words and then looked at the masseuse, who by now had become my interpreter. She volunteered to be the translator for us.

Jinalben was raised in a village that was remote and for her, Anand was a modern city. She didn't complete basic schooling. Dropped out at fourth grade and had been married off at seventeen. She came to Anand, knowing life here was different and offered more facilities than her hometown. She was happy with her husband who ran a small shop, selling odds and ends but not close to being a grocery store. In her village, when a girl was married off to a man who ran a grocery shop it was considered to be a lottery. Himesh was a nice man and that is what keeps her happy today, that he was caring, responsible and had no bad habits.

Jinalben was pregnant at nineteen with her firstborn. It was a boy and the family rejoiced at the birth of the first baby to the next generation. Her mother-in-law had raised two boys alone after her husband died of malaria over two decades ago. The mother-in-law ran a small business, tailoring clothes for women to support the family. When Jinalben arrived, she had no skills except cooking; so she began working for a wealthy family nearby as a house cook. Her husband was a progressive man for someone who only passed the tenth grade. Although he didn't go to college, he apparently read a lot and was broad-minded. One day he told her he wanted to go to Africa for work. There were opportunities there. Somebody was offering him good money to be a clerk. He was expected to keep records of sales each day, handle cash and all transactions. Himesh was good at that. They would take care of travel, food and accommodation. He went away on work and came back once in two years to meet the family. She missed having Himesh at home. It was hard, raising a child alone with an old mother-in-law and no real support system while she juggled a job that kept her away almost seven hours a day. A few years ago, Anand saw some young, healthy women lending their womb to infertile couples for economic compensation. Jinalben discovered the money they made was not small, but good enough to set up a strong business. Slowly, she began to give fodder to this idea. Himesh could come back one day for good -they would have a grocery store - they will be a family again…with comforts…

The community there was being educated by doctors and nurses on surrogacy. The details of the medical procedures, safety and how morally protected the whole idea of carrying someone's child, was, was shared with women who were interested to know. Most women who agreed were in dire need of money and the first few that came out healthy and benefited economically became instrumental in encouraging others to follow suit. Soon, more and more young couples began considering this option to get the kind of money they would not earn through years of service nor get as loans. The medical fraternity began sharing information locally among men and older family members. More men began to understand that surrogacy does not mean any compromise on their marriage. More mothers-in-law comprehended the concept. The daughter-in-law was doing this for her son after all. The woman in her was appreciative of the sacrifice. Yet, there were stories of families that turned this choice into nightmares as well. But in time, the voice of experience coming from couples who volunteered rose above those who objected. The women and their men, who went through the procedures, were the true apostles of this confidence.

Jinalben convinced her husband on his second trip, that they should consider being surrogate parents. She used the word "they" and I was amazed at how mature she was in her outlook. This was not about just her but him going through something that would change the shape of their family albeit for a while. He had equal stand, voice and partnering to do. Just as two people decide to have a child, two people came together to decide to carry someone else's child. I have never in my entire life seen such emotional maturity or witnessed profound transformation in attitude. The beauty in this situation is the contradiction, one could see at the same time. Poor, uneducated, conservative in dressing; speech and practices completely old world — but so liberated in thinking; fresh in perspective! They were radical enough to giving consent to bringing societal change!

Jinalben said she went through tests and her husband agreed to come back for good that year if they were selected. Jinalben was shortlisted and was informed of a couple they will be carrying a child for. Himesh returned and amazingly took care of her like this was their own child to keep. Her food, medicines, tests, allowances were stipulated. The doctor and the clinic took personal care of the surrogate mothers. They treated her each step of the way preparing her, informing her and setting expectations clear. They spoke to her husband regularly to make sure both were on the same page, all the way. Jinalben came back from the hospital one day and shared the good news at home...she was pregnant! They celebrated that night, making sweets at home for dinner. This now guaranteed the pot of gold at the end of the rainbow. Her mother-in-law was most amazing. She fussed over her pregnant daughter-in-law, gave her rest, told her to take it easy and Jinal said my respect for her grew with this decision because I saw she was a supportive mother-in-law who was cooperating with a working daughter-in-law. We all laughed at the tongue in cheek line. But I knew what she meant. This was a job!

The couple that came to meet her in the ninth month was Caucasian and Indian. The woman was of Indian origin, but had been working abroad for many years (at the time the restrictions were limited and couples from outside of India could come here for surrogacy which was far cheaper than anywhere else in the world. The law on that too has changed since). They expressed gratitude, immense happiness and complete indebtedness to Jinalben. The couple had been married for eleven years and were desperate to have a child. All ways failed and doctors there had told them surrogacy would be their best bet. Meeting them and seeing how needy they were – Jinalben felt the pain and the trauma of childbirth she would go through was going to be worth it. It was a God given opportunity to play God in someone else's life. Not always does one have to measure life in give and take because sometimes what we give cannot be measured. The lady had said that what Jinal was doing was priceless. No money she offered would ever be enough for what she had done for them.

Jinalben gave birth to a healthy baby girl weighing 3.3 kilograms. She had her father's light eyes and dark hair like her mother. The couple were ecstatic beyond words. She had never seen such happy people in her life. Never was a room so full of happiness as that one in which she handed the baby over to them. They didn't stay on for long. Jinalben bid goodbye to the baby girl after twenty days of breastfeeding. She had made an amulet for the little one and gifted it to the mother….a little something from the mother who carried her for nine months. A wish, a prayer, a blessing, so she would be safe wherever she be – whatever place she calls home. Jinalben in my eyes grew taller than her five feet three frame. She was illuminating us. Radiating such spiritual warmth, I was feeling small and uncouth despite my skills and clothes. She had substance in her emotions as she had in her actions.

Jinalben had moved her husband, in-laws and an entire family to think in a new way. She had defied society and compelled her neighborhood to be educated on the subject. She had stayed proud of what she was doing. She stood as a pillar of support to her husband and family all the while. She loved her own son each day more than yesterday. All this endurance of an emotional test and physical pain was for him after all. Soon her husband set up a grocery store. They began to earn better, grow financially sound and had better prospects. They were able to afford an English medium school for their son with tuitions. They set aside money to send him to college…and she had been seeing all this long ago when she first heard of the doctors and the concept. If that is not vision then what is? **Strategic thinking is attached to opportunity orientation. Visualization helps trigger motivation. Motivation is the ability to influence others through own conviction.**

Today Jinalben is the go-to person for many young women who want to consider being surrogate mothers. Her eloquence and confidence is comforting to the listener. I had one more stuck up question to ask that is usually one that comes from prolonged exposure to Indian TV serials – I asked if Jinalben's husband loves her the same way after the ;project'. She blushed and confirmed his love never faltered. Not then when she walked about with a big stomach carrying someone else's child – not now when he runs the business they always dreamed of. In fact, he speaks highly of her to his friends and family. He told her one day – "how can I look down upon someone who has the largeness of heart to pledge her body for her family and who has a soul so rich she wrings her heart to allow someone else's to breathe again?" Himesh needs a place at the altar too. An exceptionally forward thinking man indeed! Perhaps all that reading did that for his mind.

The law has changed sometime back in India. An NRI or a couple of foreign origin cannot opt for surrogacy in India. Today, the women of Anand and nearby places are surrogates to Indian infertile couples only and surrogacy is following several stringent rules. Medicine is as advanced as any country outside of India. The specialization earned in this subject has made not just the surrogate mothers here proud of what they do but also the locals who now comprehend the magnitude of such volunteering. The medical fraternity here is socially involved. To have made this possible, it would have taken some rather exceptionally skilled doctors with social acceptance to bring acceptance on the touchy subject…which is what Gujarat did seamlessly. The concept spread across many cities of Gujarat and today all have the same professional approach to the process.

At the time I visited the place, things were not as prescribed and as progressive as it is now. The government is still working on legislatives and policies that will monitor surrogacy even further. They are working on controlling the applications, eligibility criteria, remuneration and health care facilities etc. Many things will change but the women of Anand – I only hope they don't change. They are ahead of any farce. The number of educated, well-placed women and men from cities who are infertile yet closed to the idea of surrogacy will give you a permanent frown line. And then you meet these women – their community – and you can't help but smile and nod at the same time.

Desert roses are not imaginary.

My notes: On Life Skills / Management and Leadership

If you've run out of space – You are Gutching!

Jinalben in Anand was teaching a lot more than the obvious

1. A country, state or village is only as progressive as the mind of the poorest man in it.

2. Poverty and financial crisis demand drastic gear change – some that can be shocking to consider but that could elevate situations and people too, especially if it is ethical.

3. People with courage are not constricted by society and norms. They influence their immediate few to help change other minds – they don't work from out to in. They always work in to out.

4. A community or organization culture changes when leaders introduce new ideas, demonstrate the merit, communicate risk, safety and what's in it for you, just like the medical fraternity at Anand. This demands competence and faith in the abilities of who is spearheading change though.

5. Empowerment starts with COMMUNICATION. Sharing the options, the process, the whys, hows, whos, whats, the expectations and outcomes transparently allowing people to decide when they are ready.

6. Positive influence is never about PUSH. It is ALWAYS PULL. You have to draw people in to think, to ask, to agree and then to follow.

7. Decision to accept a role should lie with a well informed receiver so that it is solid and permanent with no regrets in time.

8. A strong protocol is needed to put traction on what is delegated. That ensures delegated work is well executed as per expectations.

9. Even if the country or organization does not have crisp norms around something, creating guidelines that are well translated, capacitates them to turn into a policy that all understand – like the system at the time in Anand didn't have robust laws and policies but they crafted their own to prevent exploitation and protect the people.

10. We are wrong when we make judgments based on class, position, education and the obvious indicators. If these women were evaluated for those including financial status, IQ and social appeal their ratings could be far lower than city-bred women but truth is they broke the matrix of prejudice that the women in the cities could not.

11. Human mind and its emotions don't get measured or understood as easily, which is why elements such as education, qualifications, clothes people wear and what they do for a living becomes assessment parameters. How sensible is it to hire people basis ONLY the ramifications we have made on universities and colleges?

Basis assumptions attached to A list companies to hire from? Real intelligence and maturity, ability to lead change can be sitting anywhere in reality.

12. To bring results – one has invite who is interested and not carpet bomb randomly. Who is curious will be a good listener and perhaps has an under nurtured motive that will be discovered with gentle prodding.

13. During communication for influence – talk less and be willing to listen. After you share a concept is the time to shut up and urge questions. Answer all doubts, clarifications and segregate those who are convinced from the ones who are not. Don't push those who are not up to agreeing with you. That will repel them even if there was a chance of agreement in the future. One who agrees after much caution will be more capable of influencing others. That is your brand ambassador!

14. Desensitization and detachment are not essentially bad. Where needed, they allow you the insulation required to make the right choices. One has to train the mind to detach from business and people at times. What comes naturally however is the opposite. When you know the prospects are not right, the signs are wrong and it does not look like this will endure the test of time – it is best to emotionally detach, which is preparation for severance that is unavoidable. The best way to get there is by reminding yourself of the objectives you hold in life, the others seem to hold; the reason you are here, what expectations you hold, are they met or not, if the desired end states match or they don't. Either way this is a talk that needs to happen inwardly everyday if you are not good at detachment. It will help to ensure the heart won't leap over the mind.

(14 key observations - Did you get them all or more ?)

Bias breaks the bones of human society

It does not matter which part of the world we live in, bias is a natural phenomenon that dictates and governs human choices. It is what prevents us from natural exploration and new experiences. Bias gets accepted when we fear rebuke, loss of privileges, spate of questions from others, defamation, personal insult or general opposition from others who we live with. That is conscious bias. Unconscious bias is what has always been and so it does not strike you as bias at all.

"Bias is a black, blinding cloud that looms over human communities controlling the life and destinies of many, by the will of few"

In some parts of the world, bias against women is so strong that they are condemned from seeking education, dressing as they like, driving or keeping a job. Independence in such communities is a male right. The bias stems from the insecurity of female independence and right to make decisions. Will her decisions not favoring us make our lives more difficult? Then let's subjugate her and her opportunities by preventing the very idea from entering her head. Control her head, prevent matter and knowledge from entering it; reign supreme over a mind that is now incapable of retaliation or demands. Bias is a notorious monster known to cause ruin, depletion of rights and often tends to invite inertia as a permanent ally.

When we talk of backward societies, female infanticide, rural governance etc., of third world countries make our hearts bleed. We can see the prejudice, the destruction caused by bias. We don't shirk from calling a spade a spade. The privilege of education is the ability to see things for what they are and to question every wrong in the hope that we will correct it in living time. More amazing than that is the fact that most developed countries and economies who happily see the bias of society, the oppression of women and who will clap for Jinalbens of the world, fail to see themselves as being the patrons of bias in a modern, developed economy. The dichotomy of sophistication is interesting to observe. The story of Jinal is inspirational. She was a change agent who stood against the tide to do something different that was not comprehended by her community. **The best of corporate leaders and business stalwarts will quote Jinalben's story and happily bring glory to her zero prejudice stand. But they will stand blind to the Corporate Brahmins they themselves are. Rule makers of bias and the keepers of bias - seldom notice their own shortcomings which is why the biggest lies are delivered at podiums, on mikes and in panel discussions.**

STORY 3
When a Cuckoo is born in the Crow's nest

On Identity, Conviction, Clarity of Conscience and HOPE

This is a story of a man who found he was unlike anyone else in his family, whom he could not relate to, understand nor connect with even in conversation leave alone values and purpose. This is a unique story of struggle. A struggle of a child who ran away from home to be the man he wanted to be.

India is known for a variety of cultures and traditions. The North, South, West and East of the country boasts of different communities that carry within them their own gene, personality traits, outlook and habits unique to them. Cinema in the country threw in through the tube insights into these peculiar communities. One such that catapulted to fame were the Thakurs.

Like Hollywood has an allure for Texan culture; Bollywood movies of the 70s and 80s were enraptured by the Thakurs. Thakur is a title that was given to landlords. Landlords were known for wealth, power and autocracy. Not to be mistaken for people with a last name Thakur – the moviedom Thakur is Thakur by position, by ranking, by virtue of owning vast lands. In real life, they had the power to change the lives of people - entire villages or districts for the better provided they had character. But if they didn't –they throttled people to be bonded laborers controlling money so miserly people ravaged and suffered till movies were made referring to such infamous characters.

Most movies seemed to have fallen in love with the evil Thakur idea. So they depicted them as tyrannical, highly political and dangerous. Hailing from the south of India which is less violent and territorial, I was both scared and fascinated by the idea of Thakurs – the little kings of rural lands. I always wanted to meet one in this lifetime.

This story is about a chance meeting with a real Thakur and what it brought out is straight out of the movies as well! And it is only after meeting and hearing from a Thakur first hand that I relented – movies do make stories borrowed from reality. They are not all exaggerations all the way. Like an artist has a muse…movies have one too.

Madhya Pradesh is a state I have had the fortune of traveling to, extensively. I spent almost four years hopping cities and towns here. It is arid and dry for most parts which sometimes is so barren that it is hard on a conservationist's eyes. For those who love green trees and grass, this place has much of all that lacking. While there are farm lands and agriculture they are usually located closer to water bodies. If you traverse the roads by car and drive into villages there are times you will anticipate a dessert to materialize any minute. The locals are food lovers, especially street food and Indian fast food. Cities in proportion to villages and small towns in this state are far too few so a big part of MP still carries a rustic charm. If India had a heart it would sit here – top and placed right in the center, more to the left, just like the human heart. The land here has something utterly romantic about it. Pictures could be painted here if you don't mind seeing men with guns and rifles driving jeeps pass by. Violence is common and very hard to control in some parts of rural MP. It must have been my fourteenth trip there and I had not met a single Thakur yet. For long I thought it was like going to Australia hoping to see the Tasmanian wolf, to be told they went extinct in the early twentieth century!

I cannot deny that traveling down highways summons courage especially if you are a woman. The roads at times even in cities like Raipur would have a convoy of 4X4 jeeps packed with giant sized goons who carry weapons openly. Of course I had rattled like a leaf the first few times I saw them up and close but I got used to it after a few trips.

Once I met a gang of goons/rural bodyguards in the lobby when I landed at the hotel. They began studying me, walking around me like I was a fossil specimen. Of course I changed hotel within minutes but fear has lasting effects. Then I met some enroute the Chambal valley trail right across the dessert. The driver of the cab was cool in telling me the road has "mishaps" and equal "kidnaps" so one can't be too careful around here. I was thus advised to duck and lie on the floor of the car all along the forty-five minute drive. Kneeling on the floor of the back seat of a taxi, is so much fun - time slows down to an hour in a minute. I would peep out the window, plucking whatever residual guts I had to see what these thugs look like and if I can see a real Thakur among them, somewhere but no such luck!

The driver noticed my stupid moves and said, "No bravery will work when you are staring at a double barrel pointed between your eyes." So stay down or you will get all of us killed. Some trips have been uber memorable!

I stayed there motionless, having decided to play dead especially because the colleague traveling with me clearly said if they come for us it is each one for their own. He does not have it in him to even 'try' to save me. My curiosity did get the better of me many times as the driver and a colleague made observations as we passed scenery. They, talked like ventriloquists without any lip movements. One such time I decided I just have to look up come what may. This may be my only chance to see a dangerous landlord. So thinking, I was about to pop up again when the driver corrected me – real Thakurs don't show up like this; especially not if they are the deadly type. These men are only hired snipers and henchmen or bouncers. Now, why does he need a bouncer in fields or the desert was beyond me.

Apparently landlords think and work like invaders. Their logic and strategies for expansion are the same as any of history's notorious invasions. They build army. They build means of travel. They provide weapons and train. They explore potential victims and their territories. Observe weak points. Target. Attack when the other is weak. When physical power fails, they use strategy. Lending money, forgery, dues and debts are all ploys they use to confiscate land.

Some create situations of turmoil for people with land issues. Then offer help with money and then again deploy strategy to ensure they can't pay up, extend time, double dues, tighten the noose and demand all the land the other is worth. Wars come up like that. Bloodbaths follow. Men die. Nobody will whisper. Hardly any show up at the police station to lodge complaints. These wars of groups have gone on for so long – its culture for these parts of MP's interiors. So fascinating was all this that I popped up my head again and saw them a few feet away. Men the size of Godzilla. Many of them sporting handlebar moustaches. Most wore white kurtas, some in jeans and some in pajamas, but all carried rifles and leather cross straps holding dozens of bullets. One of them screamed something as we zipped by. My blood curdled and I dashed back to the floor hoping he didn't see my streaked hair bobbing by the window. My wish to meet a scary Thakur ended in the Chambal valley.

Six months from that nerve-racking episode, I was in Bhopal, another city of MP. There was this guy about twenty-seven who I was working with on something. We got talking about Bhopal and its history with the Gas tragedy. The small group of two locals there and me just embarked on the subject of tragedies, natural calamities and what happens to people upon who such hard times befall. Everyone was sharing their experience. This guy however was quiet. Whenever someone in an actively conversing group is less involved or appears reticent, my observations automatically are directed to the non verbal signs they give. He looked like he was elsewhere, thinking about something else. I asked Sushant what was on his mind. Did he lose someone in the Gas tragedy of the 80s?

He dismissed my enquiry, stating he is not from here at all. I pressed further to see if he would tell me what got him so sentimental. Sushant said it was personal and he wanted to only listen for now. You can't prod when someone says that. The conversation, however, was enlightening and very informative on how locals handled the crisis, how those who left struggled to set up life again, the diseases that followed those who were exposed to the gas, congenital defects and the humane side of people as well. There are silent heroes in people from neighboring cities who went out of their way to help victims. The hot tea got over and so were the samosas we ordered. The conversation too dwindled and everyone got into a hurry to get home. Sushant stayed back and offered to drop me to the hotel on the way. He anyway didn't have family here.

In the car, he asked me why was I so interested in stories that are disturbing? I explained I was no seeker of trauma or tragedy; I was just scavenging for life lessons amidst everything no matter how colossal it may seem. He smiled and said now he was ready to tell me his story. He came from a village in MP, a prominent one known for wealth and violence. There were just two powerful families that lived there. One was a distant relative and his offsprings, and the other was his grandfather and sons. The brothers and cousins in these families stand together like a fortress. The first army is internal – then they recruit externally to expand. Impetuousness and extremely loyalty; these are two traits for most youth here.

Since childhood, they were taught the importance of being one, not letting the enemy gain advantage, watch money, grow money, stay connected to the people. Power and its games were discussed in the front courtyard by men of the household. This is where women were not allowed, especially in the evenings when other village men would arrive for discussions. At night the men would retire to the terrace in their huge kothi (house). This is where most of their planning and agreements would happen.

Sushant was born feeble. He was frail as a child and fell sick often. He had a full-time nanny shadowing him until he was ten. Sushant didn't get along with the other boys who were his own brothers or cousins although all lived in the same house. He preferred to stay in the company of his aunts and cousin sisters instead. The men spoke of problems all the time; of cheating, of cunning agenda, of revenge, people getting wounded, someone supposedly getting buried in a field nearby and other such disturbing subjects that usually gave him nightmares. His father disapproved his sissyness. He thought he was too weak and incompetent to handle the rough demands of a rustic life.

By the time Sushant was fifteen years old he was quite a loner. One day he was walking down the narrow path by a field when he heard someone screaming and the firing of guns. The sounds were coming his way and before he knew, it, he witnessed a chase. Two jeeps were after a screaming, bleeding man. They were having fun watching him panic and run to save his life. One jeep accelerated and two men stood up to take aim – they shot the man. The dying man turned around slightly as he fell…like he was turning about to beg for life. Life left his body in a few seconds. Sushant now clearly saw the face of the dying man – he was a cousin from the other side that was supposedly enemy camp.

He looked again at the men who killed the man; they stood there stupefied not knowing what to do with their witness; the son of the Thakur! One of them got off the jeep, pulled him by the collar and they drove off with him sandwiched between two thugs in the back seat. On the way he was mum, thinking of nothing else except he was only fifteen and too young to die. He wasn't sure if they will finish him and claim it was a stray bullet or let him go because he was family. He could try to break free and run but practically speaking there is nothing anyone can do against men this size. He looked around the jeep…so many weapons...a small country would be keen to buy them, he thought. They blindfolded him and took him someplace where a man spoke and after much shushed talk, it was decided he will be spared. Sushant was dropped a kilometer away from home and was warned by the man with a muffled voice – he cannot speak of what he saw if he wants his life spared. If they hear of him bleating ever – they will come for him. The man grabbed his hand hard and shoved him into the jeep and gave instructions on the route to take.

That hand that grabbed his wrist gave him a shudder. He began sobbing. The men thought he had buckled and was weeping out of sheer fear. Sushant was crying, but for totally different reasons. That hand he knew well. Too well. It had a large corn that scraped against his forearm. A calloused growth on the ring finger that his grandfather toyed with when thinking and often cut off with blades. It grew again and again, each time bigger. At times Sushant had been the surgeon at home to free him from that skin growth. He knew it was his grandfather. This was his family and now he was sure – murder is casual business around here. The men dropped him off on a side road. He walked that one kilometer – his life's most silent walk. When he reached home, the house was quiet and even the women were acting strange. There was a meeting that night among the men. Next morning, his father told him he was more academically oriented than capable of ever managing the family business, so it had been decided that he will go away to a boarding school to follow that up with college and MBA or whatever he sought.

Sushant then on was an outsider in his own home. Over the years having worked with corporate house and private companies, his perspectives on his own origins and background changed. On one trip, he found one of his own cousins had gone missing. Nobody knew or has heard from him since the day he vanished. There had been a murder in town, was the murmur. Either he was involved and went under or he was killed and nobody knows. Sushant didn't bother to ask or dig deeper. Two days of watching the drama at home, he knew he no longer belonged there. He had begun to abhor them more than before. The manager in him who lived by policies, rules, values, and immense communication around integrity just wanted to take the next bus out, to never return. He did just that – and never returned. Then he asked me if my wish to meet a Thakur is over. He was the product of a wild Thakur community, albeit seen as their black sheep.

I had finally met a Thakur – at least in blood. Not in ways or ideologies. His story is wound with their story. His history and his legacy is like theirs. But he chose to carve his own path although a lonely poor one for now. Sushant lived on rent; didn't make as much money as he would have had as a son in that household, nor had the ranking or power in the corporate space. But he said, "I sleep well, Seema. Never in fear. There is no worry in my heart ever about my choices. But I do worry – if karma is true, my family's curses earned will follow me perhaps. Then again, I tell myself I will get only this chance to wipe that slate. Maybe my kids will have no memory of their origin and lineage. They will grow to be tarnish free. I don't have kids today but why wait for a child – to be a better man?"

I was completely in awe of this young man and his powerful choices. In his choice, he was so alone, that when he falls sick, he has to take care of himself. When he is down he has no real family to talk to yet he was fine with who he had become. Sushant made new friends so they can be his family. He saved thirty per cent of his income for a rainy day because he knows there is no one else to fall back on. He lives frugally within his means. Over time, he turned into a good cook with all that forced practice. His personality is congenial and warm allowing others to get to know him and is self-effacing. Nothing about him indicates the wealth he was born into or his connections. Sushant could stand in a room and melt away into the dozens people there.

Just before he dropped me at the hotel, he wore this sarcastic smile and said, "I am more movie like than any movie, Seema. If you ever meet me on a Saturday when I wear a half-sleeve shirt you will see this on my forearm" he said. So saying, he pulled up his shirt sleeve and there on his right arm is a tattooed emblem – the mark of one from this particular family of Thakurs. I didn't blink for quite a while I think. It was proven – Hindi film industry sucks out real meaty details and weaves them into yarns we pay to watch. Someday he will get the tattoo removed, he said; it was a reminder of who he really is.

For now he wanted to study photography further; he was getting good at it too. Sushant travels to jungles and wilderness to click pictures of flora and fauna. Wild animals are his specialty. "One has to find what drives you; fulfils you, will keep your mind off your problems to stay immune and sane," he said. Photography it will be – till a wife and some screaming kids become the way of life. And he had clearly found an avenue, that he was passionate about enough to distract his mind and keep it strong. Such are the ways of the self-made. No complaints – no excuses – quick fixes and so much grace! He is testimony that amidst a lot of wrong can be born a right.

My notes: On Life Skills / Self Management and Leadership

If you've run out of space – You are Gutching!

He threw a few bullets – for us to bite

1. Real life can at times appear like reel life. Pain, tragedy and losses are not rare occurrence, and it is perfectly normal to feel like you don't belong in a place you are supposed to belong.

2. Some peoples have lives that are rife with drama. It would be wrong to sideline them only because too much happens in their life that we can't fathom.

3. Those that have much going on behind the scenes need not reveal that or wear that on their arm. They won't, especially if they are not the kind who are looking for sympathy.

4. At times, people are subjected to trauma and drama because of their associations and connections.

5. What we see on the outside is not them but the impact of their links and how they are trying to cope with it.

6. When you observe profound silence in someone on a subject – who is otherwise communicative, it either comes from a deep acknowledgement or simply not being attentive or interested. If it is the former, however, it usually means they have something in their memory that still rankles them too much; which is why they choose to stay out of communication.

7. People are a good judge of you as you are of them. Just as you watch them – they are watching you.

8. Others share critical life events with you, only when they know their story will be respected, listened to without prejudice, good intention and won't be misused against them.

9. Being associated with a family, company or a community that lacks morals and ethical code of conduct does not necessarily indicate one lacks depth.

10. Rule breakers and outliers are everywhere. When an outlier realizes they are one – they go in search of all that accentuates their difference and confirms to themselves the need to severe.

11. The more different a person "feels" the more indifferent they become.

12. Distance allows disconnection faster. Only the highly adaptive and ready in mind can uproot self and be okay dealing with new circumstances and less comfortable means by choice.

13. When one is greatly influenced by a leader, even wrong appears right because it is justified, like all those hired men and family members who could not use their faculties to know right from wrong.

14. A strong but wrong leader creates cults – cults that believe and strongly

fight for their belief system no matter how wayward it may be. Blind faith is what it demands. Often power and money can blind others. Else it is the artful eloquence of a master communicator who sells visions and dreams that makes the impossible possible.

15. Groups, Nexus constitute allied people who stand together to defend together and drive forth for personal gains. It also gives them a sense of fraternity, connection, bonding, belonging, protection, and with that cumulative power over others.

16. Malevolent minds enjoy the opportunity of oppression. Guilt is non-existent in conniving groups. They thrive on cunning schemes and feed on brutal confessions.

17. Challenging those more powerful than oneself is foolhardiness. Discretion is indeed the better part of valor.

18. Valor is not what we prove to a houseful audience. It is the demonstration of courage to stand and walk out alone if need be, knowing the road will be hard and lonely perhaps. If you can cut out the dramatics associated with bravery it becomes courage.

19. Once you reckon you have courage, it instantly sparks other sides of your personality that allows adventure, exploration and the guts to seek joys and thrills.

20. Being honest to oneself is not conditional. It is not what one will be when the environment is conducive, the moment is right, when a child is born, a new house is earned or a promotion announced. Changes and improvements one wishes to bring don't depend on any bell to ring. The choice you make when you have no reason is the best reason. The reason is YOU.

21. The essence of leadership begins with the ability to lead oneself before we lead others.

22. To be exemplary such that others follow you or find you an inspiration demands that you live to be that model exerting the right forces and restraints on self at all times. A leader is not someone by chair or by power – a true leader is someone with exemplary control over self and emotions.

23. Life without stress is like ocean without salt. Intelligent people reckon the mind's ability to get destructive when disturbed or lonely. They dip into their bucket of interest and pull out something they can attach themselves to strongly. The mind is engrossed that way and has no room for idle thinking. They acknowledge that the human mind is like a child we have to mind all the time. Keep entertained else mischief begins.

24. Being attached to your past, memories of the past, memorabilia, and

holding on to what they mean when they are not urging pleasant memories is destructive to self. Either detach or erase them.

25. Dissociation comes easier when there is conviction; it's not a place you want to go to ever again.

26. When embarking on a choice that will be against the usual tide – start working on financial security.

27. Improve your social connections consciously and build deeper relationships if you have decided to tread the road alone.

28. Just because we know people well, and we may owe them materialistically, does not mean we also owe respect and love. Those two are earned.

29. How you tell your story matters as much to you as to the listener. Zero sympathy and matter of fact narration means that you have begun to see your life antiseptically. You have accepted its facts and offer no excuses. Only choices concern you.

(Did you get all observations or did you find more?)

STORY 4
HEROISM: A DELECTABLE COMBINATION OF FEAR AND GRIT

On survival, tough choices, emotions, duty, compassion, courage, and honor

The next few pages are about a hero met in unexpected circumstances and her own circumstances have always been like walking on thin ice. A woman of much clarity and attachments – whose attachments the world could neither understand nor respect. She was the epitome of human strength and tenacity.

Heroes - we expect them to be enormously successful, famous, larger than life, perfect and brave. If the super human forms don't come to mind, then the heroes we know carry medals on uniform and have to their credit many gallantry awards, the President's Award or brought about some revolution that makes them worthy of praise. We are also familiar with local heroes who have earned the status by having saved lives risking their own and so heroes somehow ended up becoming a rare sighting. This is a story of a real time hero with none of the above glamour. An ordinary someone… like millions of others, but she was different. Shirin is a HERO in my eyes and in the course of this story, it will become apparent why. I remember her whenever my own going is tough; when I have to make a sacrifice and I find it hard to give in…I think of her and it gets easier to do the right thing!

It had begun to rain and the sky was pelting down rain like it was revenge. The taxi driver could hardly see where we were going. I was worried if we would skid into the ditch which lined either sides of the narrow road. The roads were bad as it is. In India, potholes appear with monsoon like pimples on a teenager's face. It's everywhere! My training program was just about done when we heard a loud, clapping thunder and with it a nuclear burst of lightening went illuminating the sky. The hotel we had organized the program in was roughly twelve kilometers away from the hotel I was staying in. Cost saving! I ordered a cab at the concierge desk to take me to where I was staying.

The place I was staying had dozens of small villa styled studios. What made it picture perfect was that the beach was just walking distance away. You open the main door and walk about a hundred meters and there began a private beach! The sound of the sea would enter the room if I left the bedroom window open. That day, there was a power cut so bad the hotels had been using generators since morning. I was praying that my room should have lights and hot water when I reach ....don't care about air conditioning at all.

The taxi finally pulled up outside a dark-looking reception of my hotel. A girl at the entrance stood with a giant lantern. Something had gone horribly wrong with their generators; the technicians were fixing it, she said so and led me to the shadowy lobby which looked eerie in the darkness. Thankfully it was open and natural light could come in, bringing with it ample breeze too.

She asked me if I would prefer to sit in the lobby until the electricity comes back or march to my room in which case she will be my lady with the lamp. I quickly mustered a vision of me sitting in a dark villa, encased in trees, surrounded by gardens, the wind whistling through the window panes and all the horror movies I had ever seen were coming back to life all at once. So deftly I told her I should prefer a lobby sofa instead. She led the way while I followed like a schoolgirl. The flickering light in her hand and her sashaying sari were a deadly combination playing strange shadows on the wall as I walked behind. There was soft music playing in the intercom or someone was actually playing it live, couldn't tell. Most Hindi cinema ghosts come like this, and then they somehow get musically inclined and sing a song to freak you out of a year's growth. I had enough goose bumps to respect the dark and the conditions of the given moment.

There was the light of dusk still trying hard to fight the might of darkness. The hotel had by then organized cute antique looking kerosene lamps, candles and some really pretty earthen lamps as well to light up the place which now in my opinion looked like a refugee camp. Rather romantic, I bemused. The lady with the lamp pointed out a comfortable seat overlooking a man-made lotus pond. As she turned toward me to speak. I was too scared to look at her - what if this is the part where she had no eyes or no features!

The dark has such profound impact on my over imaginative mind I turn into the "scaredy-cat". So I muttered a thank you and crashed into a chair; suddenly aware of tired bones everywhere in me. The chair I sitting was on had a large side table with a bright lantern on its right and some refreshments on a table farther away. Other guests were happily chatting, laughing, making the most of this sudden shut down of power. Next to my chair sat a tall, fair woman, so fair she would have passed off for Caucasian, if she wasn't wearing a chiffon sari. Should be in her late thirties, I guessed. I politely smiled at her and tried to say something so it won't get awkward. "Sure this doesn't happen often here but is exciting for some who are reveling in this change of scene," I said, indicating to a family who was playing dum charades in limited lighting. She laughed and said they have been her personal comedy show for a while now. There in that brief moment of laughter, we connected.

She asked me what got me here. And there I was, telling her the standard 4 lines. I added how my staid lifestyle and work however often got me to see places others usually frequent with spouses and family on vacations. She pursed her lips and said "some of us don't have such luck". I had been a single working mother for long and I sensed that she was either a single mother or a single woman at the least. What was the chance of finding another sister in such a castaway situation? In India, I was always the odd one out in any circumstance. Be it the condominium I live in or my work place – I would be the only single working mom and pretty much nobody comprehended the challenges no matter how hard they tried.

To make her comfortable, I told her about my two girls, the limited support system I have, my drab work to home and home to work existence, and the travel madness that distracted me in all of life's boredom. Her face lit up and she sat forward on the edge of her seat, her hands neatly clasped in her lap "We are quite alike, you know. Looks like you have struggled a lot. But let me tell you there is a lot more ahead of us. The good news about having it rough is that people who had it rough learn to seek cheer in the small things." I pointed out I hadn't yet said anything about liking small things. We laughed at the materialistic implication that I had made.

Then in a more somber voice she said, "People who go through traumatic life events find ways to be survivors. They no longer seek happiness in big things, in grand plans, they suck up happy moments and feelings from very regular mundane events and situations; like the gentle breeze blowing on your face, like a good cup of tea, like a cozy pillow on a cozy couch…". I was impressed. Those were my views! How strange it was hearing that from someone else.

In a deep voice, I heard myself introduce me to her, "Seema Raghunath, age thirty-three. Born in Mumbai – now I live out of a suitcase." She paused, watched my face intently in the natural light, smiled as she said "Shirin Kumar, age forty-three, born in Mumbai and now travel on a whim." She was ten years older but so much fun! And I was a little taken aback at the mention of forty-three because I thought she was about three or four years older. She was a stunning beauty. Spoke eloquently. Had wit and charm. There was so much hidden behind Shirin I was almost feeling happy the electricity issue happened, else I wouldn't have met her at all.

She was like a light house waiting to beam and illuminate me…if only I could get her to open up and make this evening one of the most splendid ones I have spent with a complete stranger. No better way to bring comfort to someone than to allow them a view into your own journey. So there I was telling Shirin about my own Armageddon. The battle of life in which I started with only a shirt on my back and why I live wearing a metal armor. She seemed to understand. I saw her mentally go away some place and toward the end of my story, I doubted if she was even listening.

Suddenly she said, "I am a mistress. A mistress to a much older man." She was watching my face intently to see if I cringed an inch or if I froze. Luckily nothing happened. I was so warmed meeting a fun, real person; honestly it hadn't mattered. "So are you going to get up and leave like many others do?" There was anger and some challenge in that last question. She said this to shock me. The confession jumped out of her like a dart and I was the target. It did seem rather unnecessary to me; but I regained my poise and spoke quickly so she doesn't think I am actually considering options for response. "I don't care really what you do or who you are. Who am I to judge another person's choices in life? I like how you how you speak and in this association that is all I seek. Judging is what judges do. I am not paid that much."

Something about that last thing I said made a home run with Shirin. She smiled. I had been knocking her door for a while but what let me in was this last line – that I am not judging. She calmed down and in a more relaxed tone told me she has no real friends. Like zero friends. That I am the first person she has spoken to in a long time about anything personal. She traveled to forget her past and find the motivation to start afresh.

Shirin was born to a Parsi mother and a Sindhi father. They got married late in life; so when Shirin was born they were in their late forties already. When Shirin was fourteen, her father passed away due to a sudden heart attack. That changed her life completely. There were two younger siblings at home; a thirteen year old brother and a sister who was eleven. Her mother was so crestfallen; she became a recluse who hardly spoke to her own kids. What little money they had as bank deposits were used up in the next two years to make ends meet and pay medical bills for her mother's ailments. At sixteen, Shirin realized there was going to be no money left to manage. It was up to her to fend and feed her family. Because her parents had married outside caste and community, they had no support from their respective relatives.

Many years ago, Shirin's mother worked as a personal assistant. One assignment has landed her mother an opportunity to work for a well-to-do Sindhi businessman. Shirin's father was a successful unmarried man at the time and they fell in love – got married and together created a new life that consisted of three children and a beautiful home. Every happiness they knew shattered after their father's death. Her father had several brothers. One of which was a devious man who had been eyeing Shirin's father's company for long. Being a thorough villain, he forged signatures and claimed all of her father's business and assets.

Shirin and her mother had no money to fight the case. Two years had gone by. They only had the massive house they lived in. Her distraught mother one evening told her they could still make ends meet if they sold the house and began living off the interest. A week from there, they received an eviction notice. The same notorious uncle had forged documents related to the ownership of this house too. They had two months to vacate; the notice read. Her mother went insane, crying. She was clearly incapable of thinking and doing anything. Shirin looked at the brother and sister she had. She had school to go to, two siblings to feed and send to school, plus a sick mother and no relatives. That evening a determined Shirin, took out her grandmother's shawl and wrapped it around her slender shoulders. She thought the dull grey wool made her look older which should work well for her now. She began walking towards a street known to house some money lenders.

She came across a board that said financial services, loans and funding available. Shirin went in and asked the peon to be allowed to speak to the owner. The boy at the desk was looking at her in a peculiar way. Surely it is not every day a teenager walks in as customer. Her shawl was not fooling anyone apparently! She was asked to go in to a cabin where sat a man in his thirties, tall and swarthy with a bulky frame. He had the eyes of a shark. Must be the result of working in the lending space, she thought. Afraid and obviously timid; in a meek voice Shirin asked him for a loan of two lakhs. That's what one lawyer had said it will cost to fight the case since the property was high value. He asked her why she wanted all this money.

The innocent child as she was, she blurted out her entire predicament. The death of her father, the dependents, money crunch, the cheating, now the potential loss of shelter, the need to fight the case. He laughed out loud. "You don't know how loans work, do you? How will you pay the interest and return the capital? Do you know how long cases take in India?". Shirin was adamant and fought back saying she will take up a job and pay the interest but this case is everything for them. "Who will give you a job?" he asked. "How old are you, fifteen? Sixteen?". She meekly replied sixteen and he nodded in the negative – "no scope – that's underage. There is no hope for you." And then he stared at her for a while and slowly said, "Maybe you could work for me though. Nobody will ask around here, nor will anyone know. Yeah that is one possibility. You can be my PA, I needed one and was thinking of hiring someone. It will take long to groom you but I think that's the best way I can to help you pay up the interest and principal."

Shirin was naïve. Very ecstatic and couldn't contain her relief. Her luck was going to change for the better she thought. He promised to give her two lakhs the next morning. She would have to sign documents and another one that promised she would work for him till the debt is repaid. Shirin went home a happy girl who had found a solution to save her family. Her mother was wary and too insensible in speech of late. It was apparent even to the little kids at home that Shirin was now in charge and for all practical purposes, she is their mother.

She went next morning to pick up the money. But found the man sitting there with another man deep in discussion. As soon as she arrived, her new boss said, "This is the girl. You will make the best representation you can make. Fight this case like it is mine. I want you to get your best work to the court." Saying that, he introduced him as the lawyer who was going to fight the case for her. His credentials were strong apparently and he was famous too. She felt deeply indebted to this kind man. As the lawyer left, Shirin expressed her gratitude and promised to be the best employee he ever had.

In the months that came Shirin learnt much. She was sent for classes in computers. The company also ran an exports house that sent material from India to a few countries. She began learning Spanish so it would be of use while working on projects with Spain. Her boss found her prehensile. She too, was eager to add more to her qualifications. Shirin found it hard to attend college and work at the same time, so she became an external student. This way she studied at home and gave exams externally.

The boss was kind, considerate and over time got to know her mother and siblings too. Whenever they faced a money problem; which was every month, he would step in. They couldn't make ends meet with the limited income they had after Shirin's deductions. Aman was a nice man and good boss. Shirin would not take her problems to him but he would sense it. By the twelfth of the month, they would be broke he know so he would come laden with groceries, meat, fish, vegetables, fruits, tinned food, toiletries and everything imaginable. Between all of them at home, they all actually waited for the twelfth.

Shirin was growing up and it was almost a year working for Aman. The case was catching speed and the lawyer promised another year and the verdict will be out – in their favor that too. The relationship between boss and the young Shirin was cordial, professional and yet there was something more from him towards her that others in the office could see but Shirin was blind to. On her eighteenth birthday, he took her out for breakfast and gave her the key to a car. A brand new car! It was a gift for her. She was too scared to accept. But he insisted she take it. He said, seeing her happy made him happy.

That day he told her about how he felt about her. A part of him wanted to protect her, be there for her and another part of him saw her as an attractive woman. He told her that it is usual for a man like him to feel all this at the same time and that it meant only one thing - he loved her. She was stunned at this confession. The blood drained from her face. Shirin didn't know how to react. Then he said something really kind and unexpected. "My affections for you are honest and not lewd. To prove that… I am willing to wait as long as it takes. Someday you will realize that it is best to be with a man who loves you earnestly than whoever you fancy. Between two people there will always be one who loves another more than the other loves them. I am willing to live with the knowledge you will never be able to love me as I love you. This relationship will never have the sanctity of marriage because I am married and my wife and kids cannot suffer because my large heart has found a lot of space for you. So I won't ever compel you, force you or hurt you. Someday, I only hope you will agree to be mine and for that I promise to be there for you, for your family for all that you want to do. I will be the best man I can be." So saying he dropped her home and never broached the subject again.

By now Shirin and her family had begun to depend on him to pay bills and get past each month's needs. He had started to release her salary saying he will recover when she gets her dues from the case. Over the months, Shirin began to see an even kinder warmer side of him. While she was never drawn to a man of his age or type she could not get over feeling indebted and some part of her was feeling gratitude swell big. That wrung her up.

One Sunday, her mother fell down a fleet of stairs. While carrying a washed load of clothes, she had lost her balance and tripped. She came down hard on her head and was bleeding when her brother found her. Shirin's trembling hands dialed Aman's phone number. That was the go to person in her life by then. Before she knew it, an ambulance was home, her mother taken to the hospital, tests commenced, he was paying for everything and making sure none of them had anything to worry about. Shirin's mother stayed in ICU for four days and the medical bills — she never got to see them even once! Even before the doctors handed them over, they were taken care of. That night, sitting in the corridor of the hospital leaning on his shoulder, she told him, "I am willing to be your woman however disgraceful or shameful that will be for me. I know my family needs you, my brother and sister need you…I know I need you." That was the beginning of a new life and the end of another.

A mistress was born. At nineteen, she was his mistress officially. She was given an apartment, a car, a driver, bank accounts, credit cards and a beautiful lifestyle. In return he paid for her brother's expensive schooling, college program, her sister's fashion courses and funded to set up her first boutique too. Her mother had a handsome allowance, a cook and a stay-in maid. Just about everything in life was sorted in the years that followed. The case was hard and not easy to close. In the fifteenth year since being with this man, the case finally came to verdict and it was her win. By then she was in her mid thirties, and deeply set in her life as Aman's other woman.

But things took an ugly turn when her family got their money back. Suddenly nobody needed her or him. She was the shame. A dirty story to hide. When friends of her siblings came home they would call her and ask her not to drop by. Her siblings had forgotten all that she had done. The truth about her life was that nothing she did was for herself. She had lived, she had fought, and she chose the hard road for her mother and siblings. Then when life got them to decent places nobody wanted to associate with her without appointment and sound protection!

The biggest blow was when her sister got married and kept that a secret from Shirin. She was not invited. That tore her apart. She decided that day, family — who had no need for her anymore she dint have to hang around with either. They were people, who worshipped her when they knew she was their ticket to food, clothing and shelter. Now they treated her like yesterday's garbage because they all have their own sources. **Man is an animal of needs. Those that are in need are humble on knees and when they find their spine they turn into swines.**

Aman told her not to lament about the names they call her. The abuse they hurl or the abhor they show. She did all she did because of the goodness of heart; not because she expected them to make an idol of her and throw garlands. An act of concern, a choice to help, a sacrifice cannot be measured. He in many ways was her spiritual guru too. They grew even closer after she severed from family.

Then she sighed as she told me, "He died last year of a brain hemorrhage." There was a long pause. Perhaps she expected me to say something but I had nothing to say. Wow would be harsh. So I chose to stay quiet and after long said, "He was a good man. Good is a definition of someone who is constant, consistent and clear in intention. Aman gave you a good life and loved you till the day he died. Bless his soul." She nodded and sighed again. I knew what was going on in her mind. NOW WHAT?

So I asked, "And Shirin, you travel for what?" In a matter of fact tone, she replied, "To learn, to meet, to see people, to hear, to forget, to clean my memory… if I can. Not that I regret him but this pain is because I know what lies ahead is harder than before. Now I don't have his protection, his power to insulate me and for all these years I lived in an unreal bubble only with him. Without him, my life didn't seem to have any meaning."

This meeting was long before I saw the movie Eat Pray Love. But in her story, I saw the need for a person to be reborn. To go bang themselves against the walls of life, to get strong again, to not sit there wallowing in self pity and also…go out seeking…for hope. Yes, that is what she was doing. Looking for Hope. She was looking for a sign of acceptance.

I was in awe of Shirin by now. I thought I had a hard life, but now mine looked like good desi ghee. The lights flickered and they had been that way for over half an hour. We knew electricity will be restored soon. I asked her if she felt like taking a walk to our villas. She was a lane away in another set of larger villas. As we walked, she said it felt good to talk so openly today. And I expressed my gratitude in being given the chance to be her listener. Then something pushed me to tell her that in time life will show her that prejudice is with hollow people; those with fastidious social and religious practices are also the utmost unreasonable and illogical. Common sense is alien to such people and the less they are met — the better. But few who have sound sense, no motives and definitely have intelligence on their side won't see Shirin any worse or better than a human being who lived through hard times and made the best choices available at the time. "Thanks," is all she said but said so sincerely cheerful, she didn't require more words. We bid goodbyes and went to our respective villas. I hoped to catch her before I left the next day.

That morning as I sat eating breakfast at the table a steward came to my table, checked my room number and said a lady asked him to give this note to me. I guessed it was Shirin. In it were just three lines, "There seems to be a chance that life will be fair. Not here, but someplace else like the US maybe, and with this realization I have decided to go back to Mumbai today to make preparations. I will remember you."

We didn't exchange cards, numbers or email ids. I never managed to reach her again in life even after social media platforms became big. Something tells me her last name was not really her last name but whatever it may be… I only hope, she made it to a happy place. What she doesn't know is that to me her story was one of courage, tough decisions, sacrifice, faithfulness and such emotional maturity that she made it to being one of the few people whose chance meeting in life I can never forget. A real hero!

My notes: On Life Skills / Management and Leadership

If you've run out of space – You are Gutching!

An unusual voice

1. One does not have to look as damaged as life is. Some strong people manage to keep their minds positive and with that how they appear, despite having come out of tornadoes.

2. Life's circumstances test our ability to deal with them and how we grow during them. Most of that growing comes from reactions and choices we make.

3. In retrospect, painful life events turn into a story to tell someone but the trials and tribulations when you are living in it can either weaken you or strengthen you. The story you tell years later could be one about victory or disaster depending on how you took it.

4. Nothing can be taken for granted even if the current situation appears in control and confident.

5. Known friends turn into bigger enemies when the chips are down. When the chips are down be most wary of close ones, so called allies and those who know too much. Access to information can be the unbecoming.

6. One needs to plan for adversities as much as we do for vacations and other happy events. Business needs Option B and Option C no matter how well Option A seems to be.

7. In one's absence, a world of turmoil and suffering can arrive at the doorstep that was well averted or prevented in the period of presence. When a leader is formidable, the hyenas behave. When a powerful leader is no more around, monkey business begins.

8. Enemies often do not show up until the environment is conducive for their appearance. Those that dint look like threat in any form can rise…just because there is opportunity to strike. Competition in business follows this principle.

9. Conscientiousness can be you perhaps, but to expect the world of others to think and feel the same is impractical.

10. Protection of business, of work and of assets is as critical as expansion and growth. Safety nets are a must for sustainability and a future.

11. A young person grows up fastest when there is no adult to lead them. Even in the most perfect homes – we need to provide opportunity for young minds to think independently and make their own choices. It is when we live with the repercussions of our decisions that we grow wise.

12. Youth is a period of high trust and blind faith. It takes a few burns to wake up and realize the world does not carry duplicates for parents. Parents are just like good leaders who are not appreciated till lost. And employees at times need to lose a fine manager to know the world does not make too many good ones.

13. Sympathy and empathy need not come without ulterior motives.

14. When a person is very weak, there will be many who feel the urge to help – anticipating a pay off that is more expensive than the help provided. One has to weigh the pros and cons of the acceptance. If the loss looks reasonable for the gain and one can live with the choice – it is always an individual's right to decide.

15. Being earnest to learn and to test oneself, you can take your mind away from the drudgery of life's current perils besides infusing confidence.

16. People appreciate help and sacrifice in the moment but forget it after the storm has passed.

17. To assume that beneficiaries will see compassion and support the same way a few years down the line, is being foolhardy.

18. Man operates as a creature of needs. Those who satisfy the need in the present day will be God. And tomorrow thrown down from that high pedestal when the need goes away or if a new God arrives.

19. Relationships are not guaranteed no matter how closely related people are. One can be committed to be loyal but you need two to tango without which it's doomed for failure.

20. Loyalty can be judged when the seat becomes a comfortable one. If evaluation and treatment is unchanged across good and bad times…that's someone to keep. Fair weather friends are anyway aplenty.

21. What is right today need not be right tomorrow. Who supports you and eggs you on may perhaps turn cold and accuse you later. Do not be carried away by the gregarious cheer of those who partake with you accepting a role as an accomplice. If it is something marginally unethical or immoral by anybody's books…that's the book they will hurl at you when they get bored of your favors.

22. Decisions need to be based on not just today's requirement but also factoring in if you can handle rejection, ridicule and resignation when time flips in the future.

23. When man is selfish, it does not mean he or she will be purely destructive. Love as understood and practiced by the many is selfish too.

24. It is possible to have principles and sense of duty even while clearly standing in the immoral zone. Like Aman here who loved Shirin to the zenith; stood by her through thick and thin and did all he could for her and her family until he died. True love has many forms; although only one type ends up glorified.

25. We know there are people living in the moral zone of sanctified relationships who are dishonest, who lie, hurt, cheat and are irresponsible… yet most people absolve them because they demonstrate immorality within the

confines of a moral engagement called matrimony. And suddenly it becomes not anyone's business to judge. The world is strange when it seems to have the freedom to judge all those outside of the institution though. Funnily, the world judges by the standards most tend to break anyway.

26. In comparison to shallow relationships, Shirin's would be far better albeit wrong in the eyes of society. There are those who withstand domestic abuse, mental torture, humiliation in relationships, living with very uncaring spouses yet...Shirin is who most throw stones at. Nobody bothers to focus on the culprits of sad, bad sagas.

27. When society sends to the gallows a woman like Shirin who is by definition odd, are we not condemning what is pure in her eyes and wrong in ours? Factual assessment will stay neutral to the conservative and the liberals. It only factors in conscience and personal ethics.

28. The man's wife over time had learnt of Shirin but didn't step down from being his wife because the "wife" earned more and gained more than any mistress ever could. She would lose property rights and much inheritance to come if she took this to a court and made it a case. So she lived in that marriage although it wasn't one any longer. So where does that place the moral conduct of women like this wife? Who was more materialistic, the wife or the concubine? Perhaps their need being the same made them choose the same options. But who is outside societal norms gets spat at and who is inside gets the sympathy.

29. What we conceive as right and wrong is a figment of our imagination. Very rarely do we know the whole story to pin who the wrong one was. It is only when we deliberate much that fresh perspectives arrive and that is the gift of introspection.

30. The beneficiary is always the one with power. They call the shots. Whoever is weak by need or desire will be a pawn in the hands of who has what the other needs or wants. It is important to check the ethical fabric of the one in power. Playing into the hands of one with power and no ethics can be THE END.

31. When in the path of wrong, it is easier to add more wrong. It takes an unusual person of clear understanding and clarity of mind to limit that wrong to only one. Like Shirin who in all the years was loyal and faithful to a man who was old enough to have been her father! She never strayed. Didn't take on a profession that would have further dropped her in her own eyes.

32. As people, we fail to see the good amidst what we have deemed bad. And in doing so, we dismiss the whole person along with that one thing that didn't appeal to us. As parents we do that, as spouses we are guilty of that and so are we

as managers and leaders.

33. Once a judgment is passed, it can't be washed clean no matter what the other person's penance is. Judgment is like the etching on stone – only weathering can wear it off.

34. When circumstances and people are rigid, there is no point waiting for their awakening and realization of your true value. Where you are not valued, it is best to leave while still ahead. Regret is to be saved for those who feel for you. For those who have no emotions for your feelings are best forgotten. It will hurt to severe but it will hurt even more to stay. Life is about survival. The fittest know when to run.

35. At times, new frontiers will bring the chance to breathe again, and perhaps the chance to be the real person you were meant to be minus the strappings, dispositions and conditions. Breaking free is not necessarily running away.

36. Dignity allows you the confidence to take yourself to places where you find peace. Collect your mind and prepare for new beginnings. That is catharsis.

37. Some decisions are right in a certain time and place. There is no need to overanalyze.

38. It is important that we keep in reserve the energy needed to be REBORN.

39. Even the umbilical cord is biased. To think just because they are of your parent, they will understand, value and love you forever with that same tempo is being unreasonable.

40. Even if you love them unfalteringly; and they you…it is still unrealistic to think nothing will ever change over time, be it importance or value.

41. Even in the lives of parents there are needs. Needs that some child fulfils in the moment to become their best muffin. But the best muffin crown can or move to someone else. When such a coronation happens, you must know that what they seek from you is over. Some people have the fortune of being with parents who work hard to be unbiased and very fair. Many other try and fail. Whoever said parents are flawless and the picture of perfect standstill emotions wasn't telling all.

42. Nothing is forever.

43. Wisdom lies in not expecting admiration and value from all the quarters in life. What must matter is what you do, how and when. For as long as you are right and did you best – That was the best, regardless of other people's certification.

44. After a trauma or calamity – walking away to think is not running away. Change allows the mind to find new stimulus that allows thinking from new dimensions and with that, new routes to take that would not have occurred if one

moaned sitting on the same couch day after day.

45. We hold the biggest mirror to ourselves. If that mirror shows us in fair light – it is a good life. It is indeed unfortunate if the world sees you strictly by your skills at managing perception. Your truth is known to you, like the back of your hand. If reality is far away from the portrayal…the man in the mirror will always wear a cape, fangs and throw your flaws in your face. A poor conscience often is the cause of poor health; not health itself.

46. When we don't judge people…we know people.

(Did you get all the 46 observations or did you end up with more?)

Story 5
Common sense and energy bring Radical Change

On Entrepreneurship, Vision, Determination and Willpower

A man who didn't study beyond the fourth grade went on to run a textile and embroidery company that grew to export to Europe and the US. This story is about a man who began with only the deft skill of his hand and gave a fresh breath of life to over a hundred households. His imagination and power of vision is what made the impossible, possible

Whenever I went to Kutch, I loved it each time more than the last. I had the good fortune of spending a few good days there while on work. Anyone who travels to Kutch will be mesmerized by how life is in this culturally rich and diverse place. Kutch is known for its fabulous cotton, colorfully dressed women, crafts, embroidery, soft linens too, which usually go out for exports. This apart it is known for the Kutch festival, dessert and for its migrating flamingo population. The heat – now that is something to experience! Dry, arid and skin-burning hot. The sun seems to have a special love for this place, shining all its rays down straight at Kutch. It is as consuming as it is unbearable at the same time.

It can get suffocating when summer is at its peak. The locals, you can see them eating tomatoes, cucumbers and melons of all kinds any time of the day to stay hydrated. Workmen keep a slice of onion inside the turban to prevent sun strokes. Who cares about a smelly head if it can save your life! Rock salt is in a lot of local drinks, perhaps for reason that it is cooling. So if you ever get to Kutch, it's best you do all that the locals do else vanity or resistance in adaptation can be your undoing in cruel summer.

On one trip, I decided that I will find the time to go to a Kutchi market and buy some stuff that will stay as memoirs of my trip. I wanted some of that export quality linen I had once seen. But that day, unfortunately I managed to get off work at about six thirty in the evening which was late. There was no way I could go hunt that market everyone was recommending. So I hopped into a rickshaw, (which is a common three-wheeler transport across India), and thought it is best to keep my eyes peeled for a small shopping arcade or open-street bazaar. Kutch at the time didn't really seem to have many of this kind.

A man on the street directed me to a cloth market around the corner. The place was teeming with shops. It would be impossible to comb through all these and inspect their wares. At one look they looked like the same things just hanging in different ways. Most of that confusion comes from the riot of colors. As I began walking through the hot corridors of the market, I wondered why this part of India loves primary colors so much and why so much pattern on every single article. The vibrancy is brilliant but I couldn't see all my cushions or covers at home so bright. My taste is boring perhaps — mild, light prints and pastels and this place hadn't been introduced to them. So I assumed I will find nothing up my alley here, save maybe some wooden craft.

I went hurriedly, trying to make a sweeping assessment of their stock. I then passed a store that housed some white and cream fabric which caught my eye so I stepped back and asked the shopkeeper how is that they have mild colors in the land of primary colors. He laughed at my observation and said he has a lot more where that came from.

He asked me to sit down; saying there is a whole lot of what I seek which he does not put out there on display because people who come to shop in Kutch want it to look like Kutch. Then as he sent a boy to the room at the back to get me some samples…he gave me a free education on how the desert is harsh; how lives are lost in the sand dunes; how color helps to make people stand out in all that desert brown; why the Kutchies over time got attached to brilliant colors that spark up the mood. According to him this was some kind of natural mood elevator and flashes of people in the middle easter desserts came up in my memory - all dull, all white, all layered. Then dessert people of Kutch are different indeed - guess that is why people of the world are enamoured by the spirit of India. This is the land of exuberance, vibrance, brilliance of mind and there is a bold splash of colour in all we do- everyday!

The designs in Kutch are inspired to catch the eye. Much detail goes into embroidery because everything is art here. The Kutch desert is not far away, he said, and The Rann of Kutch is a "Must do". Although I badly wanted to see both, with the flight to catch the next day that was not something I could squeeze in.

His grandfather had been a traveling tradesman who traversed the Thar many times. He believed their ancestors traveled to the extreme north of Pakistan and north of India meeting Arabs in the days of yore, to manage trade. The Arabs were the smartest businessmen of the time who mediated every products of value and sold it to Europe and other countries along the route. The Arabs and the Persians, according to him, became the price determiners. Complimenting their smart business sense was an amazing social skill. They offered much as people; great company, stories, news and carried culture with them. As tradesmen, their caravans had on them valuables, equipment, designs and products unique to the places they visited. In a way, Arabs were moving vehicles of knowledge. The Silk Route is not a casual something of mention in history. Communities associated with the Silk Route transformed their own lives by incorporating so many habits and tastes not common to their own ilk. The Silk Route traversed such that it impacted the Chinese, Arabs, Indians, Turks, Persians, Somalians, Greeks, Romans, Syrians and Armenians. Fifth to eighth century was when this old route was most dominant.

Then I wondered how his grandfather could recollect so much. He laughed out loud and said, he googled it. His own family history intrigued him so much that he went to libraries and also googled all the stories he had heard in bits and pieces. I liked this simple-looking guy with technological dexterity. He sits in a market surrounded by fabric and his love for history and geography had made him research so much that he was an archive of data.

He asked me if I knew of localization. I was zapped. A company I worked for earlier did just that for a big chunk of their work portfolio. They translated English to Japanese, Korean, Russian, Spanish, and just about every language in use. They did technical translations for the largest brands known. I didn't expect to hear the word "localization" in a shop in Kutch! He prodded me — how old is the profession of translation? How old do you think it is?

I hate to act all knowing when I am stumped. So I said I can only guess – maybe around the time invasions began? He said the first known translation was recorded around 2000 BCE; a Sumerian epic apparently. I was growing appalled at his repository. How unostentatious are those for whom knowledge is a personal journey and not a professional one! Translators performed a very important role on the silk route apparently. These multilingual agents traveled with the traders to points their language could be used and then return with another set to home territory. He said the cotton from India was weak compared to the silk from China.

After all, it was called the Silk Route because the western world wanted to acquire silk from China. China grew rich and Romans were falling madly in love with the exquisite, fine fabric that made the women look angelic. India strangely gave the most to this route but the contributions barely find mention in an economic corridor because most were cultural or knowledge based which can't be equated with commodities. Knowledge went the way to the west. What was recorded in the Vedas, Upanishads, Universities and Gurukulams went along with traders. Why did Sanskrit influence world languages? What was seated as wealth in India was what was known and recorded in sciences, architecture, astronomy, medicine and math and this was in most parts written in Sanskrit. Tradesmen regardless of which route they followed to reach India - if they wanted to learn, learned in the tongue of the land. Some carried it in bits to place they traveled thus dispersing Sanskrit as they went which infused itself in languages around the world. "India gave the Silk route and every other route much besides spices, sugar, local millets and…gold, rubies, precious stones which is what unfortunately always gets talked about," he said.

Strong ginger tea arrived and I got comfortable, nestled in a bamboo-and-jute chair which had colorful cushions. Subconsciously, I had begun accepting that so much color is not too disturbing. Besides, I was feeling festive in the conversation with this man that sparkled my dulled brains like fire crackers. I knew the mood elevation was directly connected to this wonderful walking encyclopedia, sharing freeware data.

He continued, "It was a baton exchange trade route. One rarely would travel along the entire route. One man's produce or products would be purchased by someone else at a pit stop from where he continues till he sells to the next until it reaches end user. It seems the Roman senate had prohibited usage of silk and published bans, but nothing worked. Silk was so popular that at one time people would kill for silk. After the trip many days later…I researched on his claim and found that all he said was true!

The Roman law designers abhorred silk and thought them to be decadent and immoral. This is what they wrote…"I can see clothes of silk, if materials that do not hide the body, nor even one's decency, can be called clothes... Wretched flocks of maids labor so that the adulteress may be visible through her thin dress, so that her husband has no more acquaintance than any outsider or foreigner with his wife's body."

I was impressed by this man's deluge of data long before I validated them to be right. He spoke so confidently, there was no doubt in my mind of his accuracy.

I had to ask him – why is he stuck here when he should be out there teaching some place or leading a big business house. He delivered an unexpected thunderbolt **"Who says intelligence or capacity to store information equals success? Because success is also as much about being at the right place at the right time. Opportunity is about knowing one's turn – Carpe Diem – seize the day. Many aspire and for some, even their best does not reward much. One must wait. Patience is a virtue. To be upset and angry because you didn't get your due is the devil at work. Don't let the devil take over."**

He spoke to me like I was five years old and will be imagining a gargoyle with horns and claws, which incidentally I did. When we leave our mind in the hands of dejection, that sense of doom becomes so real, we miss any shape or form of good cheer in store for the day. Hope, on the other hand, is so brightening – we sit in anticipation of what it will bring next. It evokes a tendency to anticipate what you have been waiting for at the sound of a knock or any mail. Hope is so powerful it kills disappointment.

Just then, like he was reading my mind he said **"Keep hope next to your pillow each night and see how you will wake up the next morning. Whatever you sleep with, is what you will become."** This man personified everything he spoke. As I listened to him I visualized a scary and angry, ogre for disappointment and I also had attached a bright, handsome face for hope. He should have been an animator, I thought. Suddenly I sensed time running and wanted to get back to the hotel. Before I could ask him again to show me the light colored material that was in stock, came the helper loaded up to his neck with different fabric. The finest, soft, cotton I ever touched in my entire life! The duvets and the bedspreads were fit for royalty. If only they had wide selection. So I lamented the range and expressed my appreciation for such classy work.

He seemed surprised and said there was a lot more of this kind just that they have more value as export material but don't sell as much in the local market, so obviously the display is less too. He hoped to start exports someday. That is where the big money is. The work seen on the traditional products were made by hand. He has over a hundred women and men who work on different forms of art and craft. He went on to tell me how he started as a skilled embroidery expert himself. His father had lost a lot of money gambling and his generation began dirt poor. While they lived on the memories of the riches their grandfather and ancestors before them enjoyed; it fuelled his ambition.

He was ready to rub his nose in concrete if that's how he would bring back the lost family glory. A few artisans had approached him and urged him to represent them, sell their produce because he was well connected. Soon, he garnered a good hold on what customers wanted, incorporated the change and began designing himself without any formal schooling. He learnt textile chemistry through participation. The number of people wanting to sell via him grew. He was selling all over India and across the border to neighboring places like Nepal, Burma etc., through agents.

I suddenly remembered a man I had met at Baroda market in Gujarat who was quite impressive just like this man I was now talking to. Just like him, he worked on fabric and weaves. The difference being he using machines. He had moved to fine design and usage of silks. Shyam was his name. Shyam had met a German one day at a conference he went to. In his simple functioning business, attending conference and expos was tad too much. But curiosity had taken him there. There were many sellers of different adjacency products and all that aided the textile industry. One kiosk was selling advanced machinery from Europe that did splendid patterns, stitches and reduced manpower, also giving an option to do part handwork. Not that I understand the technicalities of this line but I narrated what I heard and how the Shyam in Baroda had purchased several machines on loan. Today, he is a successful exporter. The owner was nodding – smiled, looked up, "like I said, when it is your turn, you will know." So saying he left me to his attendant and I picked up some stuff, feeling weird about his sudden loss of friendly banter. At the cash counter, in an inattentive way he collected the money I gave and told me to come back tomorrow – more stuff like the kind I like will be on display. For me apparently. Sweet!

There was a store selling home décor and I wanted to pick up some things from there, before leaving the market, so I went in. The flight was in the morning and I had all packed my bags; so telling myself that there is no need to worry, I convinced my guilty mind – I had more time to shop. As I sat there checking out what I came for, a boy came running in from outside. He was someone's store help. He asked me if I had been to the shop that was about twenty feet away just now. If I had met a man who I discussed machines with. I confirmed it was me. He dashed to the landline phone in the shop and in loud brash sounding words informed the person at the other end that he had found me. The owner from the store who I just purchased things from, came in hurried steps, sat down next to me on the diwan in the store and said he just has to talk to me.

Most store owners in markets like these are like brothers. Accommodating and adjusting with each other. He implored if I recollect anything about the man from Baroda. He wanted to know more and hoped to speak to Shyam. I didn't recollect his full name or anything valuable to give him the lead. With just a first name you can't hunt someone in any city of India. Dyslexia has often interfered in my ability to recollect names. Then it struck me that I had a card back at home. Maybe if I could find that, I could connect these two men. He urged me to help him somehow. He asked me to stop by his store on the way. I did. He gave me his coordinates and told me a dozen times at least that he needs to connect to the man from Baroda.

In a bag sat a neatly-folded, white, super soft quilt I hadn't purchased. He gifted this to me saying he had the most illuminating discussion and that I should consider this a gift for stimulating his mind. I wasn't comfortable with that. Seeing I wasn't okay with this he asked me to pay him one rupee if that sense of "free" was stopping me. My resistance was plain. Then to convince me, he got his wife, a shy village woman. She spoke in kutchie – something I couldn't fathom. The owner explained – he translated. "He has been waiting for a sign. The calling he has been anticipating for is perhaps now in Baroda. And through this man he may learn something that changes his scope and his destiny." I so wanted to help the two men connect. Upon my insistance his wife accepted some money, and I returned home with a beautiful quilt plus a homework.

Of course, that is what gifts do – they linger on the mind and create indebtedness. He had succeeded in staying on my mind with that. I hunted my house, every nook and cranny till I found that card finally. I called him and gave him the coordinates. Then somehow that cloud of burden reduced after I hung up. I clearly stated I can only introduce people -not guarantee any real outcomes. He is the leader of results and his tomorrow. So saying, I washed my hands off the whole case and breathed easy.

I had forgotten the whole incidence. Seven months later, I got a call while I was on the road traveling someplace. It was him telling me how happy he is and grateful too, for that connection did bear fruit. He not only met the man in Baroda, but also spent twenty days there, saw the machines in action, stayed on to watch the demo of a new variant, check produce, quality, quantity, and servicing etc. The man I introduced him to turned out to be a good-hearted teacher. Got him introduced to a bank and helped secure his loan as well. Each of those machines cost 16000 dollars or approximately 15 lakhs each. He secured loan to buy several machines. For the next three years, he was going to work exclusively for Shyam- supplying to Baroda. Shyam had a demand that he could not supply all by himself. So with that existing market they had shaken hands to partner together. He was going to sell to Europe and the US! His flair for designing was back to the forefront. In fact, what he was doing now had received outstanding feedback making him unique in the space. He was calling to say thank you for a chat that changed his 'stuck in a rut' phase. Time has finally brought him to live his long held dream of being a designer and exporter.

I never heard from him after that. There was no need to. I am sure he rode the tide and I take "no call ever after" as an indication of success. Success is very absorbing and engaging. People always find the time to cry, lament, and then call to complaint or curse their stars. But when the going is good – there is so much to do, one can't blame a successful man for not remembering to call. A hard-working man that he was, the opportunity must have consumed him with work and joy simultaneously. All that ends well sometimes ends with SILENCE.

My notes: On Life Skills / Management and Leadership

If you've run out of space – You are Gutching!

Between words

1. The idea – when in Rome live like a Roman is not only contextually right to being a cultural fit but also applies accurately to survival skills. In doing what the locals do to adjust, you adapt better. Locals have mastered knowledge on what works best in their geography and socio-political structures. If it does not clash with your sensibilities, it is good for you as well and that is the spirit of the TRUE TRAVELER.

2. People with worldly wisdom and meaningful learning exist anywhere. They will not come with the usual qualifications, but common sense, life philosophies and general knowledge will set them apart from the common educated masses. It is our bigotry that expects all intelligent, capable visionaries to be sitting in the board room.

3. While a large portion of small town talk can be gossip and bunkum it is possible that somewhere among them is an uncut diamond. Someone so well attuned to the working of the world – they have gained knowledge that can make you relook your own qualifications. Keep judgment at bay when you leave home.

4. A traveler is a veritable representative of their country or state. They are moving brand ambassadors; who are expected to mirror the cultural beliefs and human values of their home town. All the people a traveler meets will form opinion basis how the traveler is experienced by them and others. The traveler is the summary of the place they belong to. A traveler has to be more responsible as they travel outside their home country because brand responsibility gets bigger outside home territory.

5. Savvy is someone who changes with time. Who accepts what comes as new will demand new skills and will endeavor to befriend the change. Staying alien to technology, for instance, would have this small-time businessman limited in thinking like the rest around him. Resistance to change makes one a career prude. Skills open doors to new knowledge and knowledge to success.

6. People are less pompous and more genuinely passionate about sharing knowledge that comes from personal interest. While knowledge gained from professional pursuit is egoistic because it is connected to opportunity, growth, scope and competitive standing.

7. But when some knowledge that is acquired from natural interest and inclination has to be shared 1) It will be delivered to only a willing mind, 2) The assessment will be sharp to sift the strong listener from others, 3) If at all a burst of information does gush out, it is not to impress but to share and impart information quickly because the moment and the person is valued. An absorbing sponge has

been identified!

8. Intelligence need not indicate success. Being the proud owner of an elephant's memory, hoarding several TB space of data, does not impress the world of humans – unless that memory and knowledge finds an APPLICATION.

9. Success is also about recognizing the right moments of chance. Right people. Right connections. Right things to say. Right proposals to make.

10. If change does not arrive by staying put, then move. Throw yourself in places that are unusual and different. The right place and time will be somewhere there.

11. To wait for the right opportunity to come knocking on your door would be like sitting at a café, hoping a film producer sees your bright beautiful face and then begs you to be his next lead. Because in your face he saw an entire script comes to life. It will just as highly unlikely as that!

12. Impatience that is unrequited by opportunity often results in frustration. For many people frustration that lingers for long is followed by visible agitation.

13. Once frothing anger is given room, it occupies all the corners of your life. Whether you are upset over your pace of your career /business or lack of momentum in personal relationship – the thing you don't have and that you seek begins to occupy the mind; leaving no room for anything pleasant.

14. This consumption slows down the individual further. When you don't succumb to disappointments the free room in the mind allows you to stay creative, toy with ideas, mingle, meet people and often that is how change arrives.

15. Being cheerful despite the odds is not easy but not impossible either. It only depends on what you are paying attention to. The crying child in your head or the laughing one. If you begin to pay attention to the positive side of life you will find ample simple joys. Like chatting with a stranger, sharing a drink, meeting a friend… whatever. It keeps the mind off its bemoaning habit. Positivity begets positivity.

16. Hope is a power house. An indestructible energy that can only be killed by the individual themselves. Anyone who accuses others of killing hope is bullshitting. Hope is like a personal pet. One that is fed, maintained and kept by the owner. Its destruction is self-made too. And its price is paid by the owner and at times people associated with them. That is how destructive depression can be.

17. Hope is to be practiced. It is a conscious reminder needed through the day and especially at night to calm the mind and allow the subconscious mind to invite good thoughts and perceptions that will automatically receive the next day with much warmth. Hopeful people are happier people.

18. Curiosity always pays. It takes one to new doors that were thought to have never existed.

19. Allow yourself to meet fresh people with different ideas from yourself; the more unlike you are the more they will stir you and teach you.

20. Be open to new roads. Unless you allow yourself to risks and experiment nothing new will arrive. Shyam went to a conference against his grain but that was a business game changer. One that affected the protagonist of the story as well much later.

21. One man's curiosity that is rewarded can change the lives of people around them and also people far away who may be inspired by them.

22. But remember, one man's curiosity impresses only people equally curious. If the search for something different and the guts to TRY does not exist – you will never recognize the SIGNS.

23. It is your duty to acknowledge the right time, right place, right people. Once you do – seize the day. Now is all that is real. The tomorrow dialogue is for procrastinators and losers.

24. Do all that you need to that will influence people. The day people reckon your ability, remember your work gets easy, because they believe in you and you don't have to convince anyone too much. People will seek you for help and at times to help you. You have to bring out the best of your genuine side to be able to register as a profound entity in other people's minds.

25. Sometimes, who teaches you will also be taught by you, although unintentionally. Like, I was learning from him and something I said happened to be what he was keen to learn about. A chance. A coincidence. That is how the world works. Who gives will also be the one to receive.

26. We are exchanging valuable, priceless lessons, and chances as we pass each other in the hallway of life. Everything is quid–pro-quo. Sometimes we gain in kind that impacts spirit, our views and attitude. At other times, it could impact solid areas like business, money, assets etc.

27. Material success has a seed. One that is set in a very abstract collection of values and personal orientations. These values and inclinations support radical thinking and courage. We don't see it because it is intangible but sense it when we meet such people. It is this set of tools that convert ordinary people into leaders.

28. Natural intelligence is nothing like the practiced, thought molded, formatted intelligence we commonly know and come across. Natural intelligence is more rooted in one's primal senses and instinct. It is based on aptitude and interest. It is not systematic or methodically grown. It finds its avenues for gaining

information from unlikely sources.

29. Trained intelligence follows model patterns and has rather predictable interests too. Most highly successful people are naturally intelligent. The best indicator of natural intelligence is a person's ability to grasp any subject, however unallied or unrelated it is to their life and profession. People with this ability fathom things quickly and ask many annoying but extracting questions. It lays the foundation for them to build their concepts on new subjects they are getting acquainted with. Learning agility is the corporate usage for this skill.

30. One of the traits of people with high learning agility is that they possess an ability to rake up some poignant concerns, points and issues in areas that were just presented to them. It will appear like beginners luck to others or plain fluke but what it really is, is an ability to travel super fast and catch up with many who master the area. Leaders need this ability without which their survival is dim.

31. Pretentious people wear their knowledge on their sleeve dishing out anything and everything they can remember, loving the sound of their own voice. That is the biggest giveaway of a formatted mind. Natural intellect also carries the intelligence to demonstrate its bearings, but they do so with only good receivers – at appropriate times. This comes from the fact that they have a strong sixth sense developed in reading people.

32. Success is more demanding and time consuming than failure or lacuna. The heady sense of being in demand and having to attend to many facets of work and life does make it hard for successful people to socialize without a cause.

33. However in the case of intimate relationships — success cannot be an excuse for being inattentive and uncaring. Great losses through failed relationship and friendships await people who allow success to go to their head. In time, loss of valuable people and advice that can ground a person becomes the reason life turns shallow or a downfall begins.

(Did you get all 33 observations - or did you find more? Then you are getting better at this)

Story 6
Punched out by the Obnoxious

On Character, Values, Perception, Reality and Stoicism

A man dreaded and feared; highly successful and powerful; whose reputation entered the lane before he did was nothing like he appeared to be. The world perceives the tough coarse man as the big BAD GUY. This is a story about a man who was irony - personified. Presents to us why perceptions matter and how we can be devoured by angst.

I had some teaching work at Gurgaon; a wonderful city of beautiful houses and bungalows. If we are not discussing the subject of safety and security for women, then this is a wonderful place to settle down. This city earned itself a bad name on eve teasing and harassment of women but is changing for the better. So I was on an assignment that had me parked in a guest house for over a month and had to get to Delhi or Noida for work, since that's where the two clients were. It was a comfortable, cosy, really well-designed bungalow. It was supposedly owned by a non resident Indian; who I could see had good taste. It had been converted to a guesthouse only a year ago after the family went back on work. This spacious house came with a set of staff, a cook, a full-time manservant for cleaning and odd jobs and a gardener cum security guard; besides a washerman who came and went on the basis of his washing duty.

For almost a month, I was the only guest there and had the whole house to myself. There was a long veranda lining the three bedrooms at the back, which did not face the road. If you sat there in the evenings, you could kill time staring at the garden and its trees that housed several types of birds. The verandah overlooked the neighbor's backyard; but there was a simple divide between properties created by growing a creeper over the wooden fence.

Every evening as I sat there and peered over, in-between the gaps, I would see two kids playing. They had many adults supervising them. The high-pitched warnings came from the grandmother who would scream out what they shouldn't do. I used to be happy to settle down on the bamboo sofa placed on the verandah after a long day's work. Warmed by a cup of tea, listening to the drum of their domestic life – I would borrow these sounds to calm my nerves. By pretending the sounds belonged to me, that wonderful "family noise" became what I came back to. My own children were at a boarding school at the time and this is how I coped with all that heartache; by watching other kids play and cherish their voices.

The little fellow must have been seven or so, and played with a ball that he would strategically land into the lawn of the guesthouse. That was a signal for me. He was bored and wanted to talk across the fence. I would stand by the fence, asking silly questions, pulling his leg, sharing a laugh until someone called him home. This friendship grew and the gardener at the guesthouse too would join us at times. He was an old man from the far east of India who loved to speak in broken English. Most days I was forced to tell a story so I had two in my audience in rapt attention. The kid, and the old man who was as childish as the kid.

The girl was smaller. About three years old and inseparable from her mother. Any sight of a stranger and she would run away like she saw the yeti. The boy was desperate for fresh faces and the gardener desperate for anyone who would allow him to do nothing. He would smoke and sit on the tuff of grass to listen. Mandy – that was what the boy was called. It was probably short for Mandeep or some name like that. Mandy would ask questions, breaking the flow of my stories and every time I answered or explained — the old man would say, "I gutching." (I getting) to confirm he is with us in the story. Some evenings, our story would break unceremoniously because another decibel had arrived in that household. This voice could freeze anyone's flowing blood. Mandy's father. I was mortified of him too.

As soon as Mandy's father's car could be heard in the lane and Mandy would fidget uncomfortably. In response, we would break up, agreeing to continue the next day. At times in the late evenings, I could hear Mandy's father – Bikram pacing the backyard, talking to people on the phone. Yelling and demanding as usual. There was only one pitch to his voice. Loud. One Sunday afternoon, I had gone to a local market to eat something different for a change. There is only so much paratha I could enjoy but telling that to the cook, who prided his twenty-seven varieties of parathas, was hard. So saying, I was going to get some shopping done; I had escaped from eating more parathas. Having finished my meal really fast at a fast food restaurant, I couldn't see anything else I could do, so I hopped into a rickshaw and got back.

Seeing me back so soon, I was sure the kind cook would make me his world famous parathas again. So I decided to walk around the bylanes a bit and kill time. I was appreciating someone's horticulture skills by standing outside the bungalow, paying attention to the well trimmed hedges, even grass, the flower-lined cobbled pathway…when I heard a skid and some noise. A kid had rammed into a passing bike or it was the other way around. He was thrown off and hurt. The biker fled. I ran towards the kid and long before I reached there, I could tell it was my new friend Mandy. He was bleeding. His calf was torn with a spoke of the cycle's wheel having ripped it. I can't stand the sight of blood but this was no time to faint. I needed help to get him home because I had no clue where doctors would be in this unfamiliar city.

A car passing by stopped and the elderly couple in it stepped out to help. They fussed over him so much, the little fellow who was being brave until then suddenly turned into a lost pup. He began howling even more when he saw the blood and I had a hard time trying to calm him down. We tried to tell him we need to take him to a doctor as soon as possible. There was a good doctor nearby, the old gentleman knew well. One of those rare doctors that work on Sundays. But the boy was crying for his mother by then and wouldn't agree to go see the doctor. I told the old couple that I know him; he lived next to the guesthouse I was in. I could take him home but can't carry him and his cycle. The kind couple offered to drop all three of us. By then, the cycle had become an entity. So off we went. Mandy was a very handsome boy and despite his tears and dirty clothes, he was as charming as ever. I told him how dashing he looks despite being hurt and he slapped my hand to say knock off the bullshit. Then he smiled for a bit. Vanity gets everyone all the time.

We reached his house and suddenly it dawned on me that I would have to meet his scary father. Staff at the guesthouse had told me that he was a powerful man coming from a family of politicians. His family has been in it for decades and generations. He, however, was highly educated unlike the usual politicians in India. He had good innings in career; had a good job, lot of investments, and good connections. He was so formidable that it was hard for others to befriend him. The frightened neighbors chose to give him the cold shoulder because for them it was like being caught between the devil and the deep sea. Bikram was six feet three or so. Built like an Ox. With a voice quality that would have got him a job at any palace as the announcer, who didn't need a loudspeaker.

I had heard him threaten some guys over the phone on some nights while I had my dinner. That spoilt my appetite those nights. I had imagined the recipients of his verbal lashes to be thin, stringy, meek, voiceless people who cringed in fear of him. The cook had told me a story of how one day Bikram smashed three guys single-handedly in their lane at night. There was a lot of hullabaloo but no one ventured out to see or to meddle. He was dangerous. As I stood outside Mandy's house, all the gossip I had heard from the cook and the watchman came back in a flash. Before I could ring the bell, he arrived at the gates. Bikram had probably heard the sound of a car, many people step out and the clanking of a broken cycle. I was gulping hard.

The house was built such that it was closer to the front gate, allowing more room at the back and the sides for privacy, also providing safe playing spaces for the kids. He scooped his son in a flash from the old man's hands and invited us in as he walked ahead. The old couple, I am sure, were in the vicinity and knew much about him to make an excuse and flee. I couldn't call going to the next house fleeing exactly. So at lightning speed, I processed options for me to bail out, but before I could say anything, his tall, sophisticated beautiful wife came to the garden. She was frowning and looked obviously worried. I quickly told her what happened and how I found Mandy and that he wanted to see his mother and not go to the doctor right away. She nodded and asked me in — gently moving me in by my shoulder. Now excuses won't be decent. Servants flew in from all quarters.

The house was massive. Much bigger inside than it looked from the outside. Now I felt like the poor neighbor given a peek into the life of the rich and the famous. Funny! That guesthouse wasn't even my house but I was humbled by the opulence of this house. Anyway, I was asked to sit and Monica, his mother, called their family GP over to their house urgently. Mandy was taken in to wash his wounds and I was thinking of a way of getting out when Mandy was demanding to be brought back to the living room because he wanted to sit with me. Funny boy, I thought, when he is with me he wants mommy when he is with mommy he wants me. Men will be men! Internal humor over, I saw myself distracting Mandy, while his mom tried to clean his wounds. She thanked me profusely for being there for her son and getting him home.

That's when Monica learnt of our friendship across the fence. She seemed happy that he was making friends despite the obvious age difference. Apparently he didn't get along with kids his age at school. The doctor arrived and looked tad pensive. He said Mandy will need stitches immediately and that he will have to be taken to the clinic for the small procedure. His mom drew in a deep breath and his father shot her a look of warning that said, "no melodrama please." I was so scared that I was willing to agree all human emotions are unnecessary manmade creations. Well, she locked all her motherly feelings in an iron vault and stood there motionless. I was waiting for this scary man to leave with Mandy so I could vamoose. As soon as they left, I took my leave gracefully, however, Monica asked me to stay. She looked like a nice woman to talk to I had no friends here to make the stay interesting. I would have liked to chat with her but Bikram was a worrisome item. I didn't want to take any chances, so I told her the staff would be worried over my long absence; that she should come over and join me for tea till they all come back from the clinic. Agreeing to the idea Monica followed me to the house across. Humble or whatever, this house had a warm inviting air about it. As soon as I got in, I felt at liberty to all host all types of feelings again. Overbearing personalities and control freaks can do that to you – dismiss your right to free emotions.

We sat down on the sofa in the verandah and she asked me about my life, work, and what got me to Gurgaon, noticing I was not from the north. She was a beauty pageant winner for a state. She was among the top five for Miss India. She looked it even now, I mused. Monica had met Bikram when she was at the crest of her career and dreams. He wanted to marry and settle down soon. She was at crossroads. Either marry the man of her dreams or continue with her career and hope to meet another man of her dreams. She thought that was highly unlikely and sought her grandmother for counsel. That old lady who was ninety at the time told her that is a decision only she can make. If career spells her identity; if exploration and indulging the mind is her kick; if she derives energy through intellectual pursuits or challenges — then a job will be stimulating. But if she is more heart than mind and wants the joy of a wonderful man's company, the security of his presence, and that security is a must for her to flower and be who she must be then it means good matrimony will be her fort from where she will shoot her best arrows into the work of career and progress. I hadn't seen things that way until that day. Having heard feministic ideas at its extreme end and having seen enough women weakened by only domestic existence — this explicit middle path was a new one for me.

Monica has a job and was doing well. In fact, she was as successful as Bikram. No wonder that house looked as snazzy as it did. He had estranged relationships with all his family. She meant the world to him and vice versa. They were the ideal couple; the kind books write about, I thought. He was all that she wanted in a husband, she said, and that decision she made then as a young model, turned out to be her best. Now I was burning to ask some questions but thought it would be inappropriate. Something about my expression gave away too much and she asked me if I had a contrary view then I ought to share. She wouldn't mind.

I told her I was terrified of her husband. All that she was telling me about him being caring, responsible, sensitive, humane etc., seemed contrary to all the yelling and screaming I was hearing from him in the evenings. Or the perceptions the neighborhood held of him. She dipped into quietness for a bit before she spoke and then rather indignantly said, "Nobody understands him because he never made the effort to be understood by others. And in that, he is at fault for not mingling. They assume by what they see and hear but who and what he is, is completely ironic. What matters most to him is me and the kids, and that is his most natural side – the kindest."

I must have looked skeptical so Monica went on to tell me why she fell for him. He was twenty-seven and she was twenty-one. He was working at a plantation someplace tucked in the hills, where there were tribals and much poverty. For the first few years they were just good friends although both harboured feelings for each other. He did most of the work by himself. Although raised in a home where a spoon appeared when he demanded one and water was served by a maid; in this hamlet in the woods,, he was one among the tribals.

Bikram only had one help. He used to get his clothes washed and ironed by a lady down the hill about two kilometers away from where he lived. She walked all the way to pick up and deliver the clothes to him. The few occasions he had gone to her small stall where she ironed with charcoal and a giant old-world iron – he used to see two kids playing in the dust, mud and coal, blackened beyond recognition. Her husband had been knocked dead by a train. Ever since then, she took over their ironing business.

This one time Bikram didn't get his clothes back on the scheduled Wednesday. Another week went by and he decided to stop by the stall. Upon enquiry he learnt the lady had fallen seriously ill and was taken to a municipal hospital. Some neighbors were looking after the kids and for the first time he saw the tiny faces, actually clean. A cute boy and a girl. He handed them some money for aiding hospital bills and went home.

Three days from there, one afternoon a little boy was loitering outside his house. Bikram recognized the washerwoman's kid and asked the boy what he was doing so far away from home. He said he had come to inform him that his mother had died and he cannot identify his clothes from others and that Bikram would need to come to the stall to pick them up in person. Bikram was taken aback how matter-of-factly he spoke without a tear. Poverty at times makes people think and speak factually minus of overt emotions. The kid's dedication to complete the pending job, persuasiveness to find the house on the hill – all this was as amazing as it was touching.

Bikram did not sleep that night. He went to the office HQ next day which was a few kilometres away. He located the school that his company was funding. He had heard they have a boarding facility too; checked the cost of education and stay. He then came back to the foothill and met the locals. He proposed to pay for the kids till they would complete tenth grade — till they were at least sixteen. The villagers were only too happy to get the kids off their hands. That night he came home with two lost sheep. Both were mature beyond their years. They wanted to help him wash dishes, sweep, clean, make their own beds – they were ensuring that they were not a burden. Bikram's heart went out to the orphans who still minded their manners and valued kindness despite poverty at a time their losses surpassed anyone's understanding.

Bikram became the guardians for the two kids. He was only twenty-four at the time. Monika and Bikram wrote letters to stay in touch at the time. When he met Monica few years later — he was an acting father/big brother. What made her fall in love with this ginormous, dangerous appearing guy was how inversely soft his heart really was to his exterior.They were deeply in love by the time. Bikram asked her to marry him ONLY if she would be a mother to the kids he had adopted– this was an irreversible condition. Monika was delighted to accept the kids Bikram already had.

After they were married, Monika met them before they set out on their honeymoon; she wanted to be a part of this in a meaningful way right from day one. Whenever the kids came home on holidays, she was their mother. And when they visited the kids every quarter, they went laden with utilities, gifts and toys like any parent visiting kids in a boarding school. Bikram had saved money for them and was saving for a rather wholesome education that budgeted post graduation/ MBA too. Monica's big, brown eyes looked at me and asked "Anyone who can love hapless children can't be a bad man, can he? I don't care what others think or say, I know Bikram is unique." By then I felt so guilty for making all those sweeping statements about this man – I had difficulty swallowing. So they were parents to two orphans long before they had their own kids! I could only imagine.

I asked her as politely as was possible what that ruckus was, a few weeks ago in the street. He was beating up some people. Does he do that often? This I guess was the part that needed explanations so my willingness to accept my assumptions could be improved. I was subconsciously trying to pull something out that proved he was a rogue indeed.

Bikram had beaten up two men a few nights ago. That was true. One of their housemaids had gone missing. He had found two men had something to do with that. The men were suspected of running a racket where they lure young hired helps to move them as illegal migrant workers to other countries where they get exploited in every way imaginable. Bikram got the maid back and the two men had landed home demanding her return. He punched their lights out, put them in place and to ensure they never return, filed a police complaint. In fact he was helping the cops identify the men and erase such rackets. I didn't know what to say.

Monica said the world misunderstands Bikram because he does not bother to explain himself. He allows people to believe what they want to and so everything he does is observed far more minutely but because of that it also means people can weave what they want and have something to gossip about. She was a happy wife. The kids knew daddy does not like them talking to strangers and so they scurry when daddy comes, not because daddy was a bully. Their daddy protected others from bullies. He was loving man whose world revolved around the family.

His yelling and screaming in the evenings was mostly about his family trying to get him to pay up some of their debts and burdens. They ran for elections and lost. The dues had grown and wanted a scapegoat. When he never ran any political campaign and steered away from that stream; he didn't want to have any part in it now. They emotionally blackmail him all the time and the soft-hearted man he was, he would listen and get worked up. There was reason – there was logic and there was a pattern showing up. He was a lion outside and a mouse inside.

I was stupefied. Amazed at how we see people on the basis of a few signs and then rely most on tell-tales from other people to form an opinion. An intimidating persona keeps most people at bay. And people with intimidating countenance also often come with the resolute nature of being unyielding. That damages them further. They are left with only a handful who know them and since those few are all that matter to them, the perception never gets corrected.

The game of lion and mouse is not understood.

There are some people who are lions outside and a mouse at home with those they love. With those at home there is no ego and they are willing to give in but are relentless outside. The other who is a lion at home who chooses to roar at all those with whom they share guaranteed relationships because no matter how sadly you treat family; they have nowhere else to go. You don't divorce or quit parents, siblings, or even spouses easily. But this roaring fierce lion is a mouse outside. one that steps out to meet and greet others kindly whose opinion matters. They are attached to their social image. Such people believe image is built and maintained not by family but by the community and with that premise the best of them end up as part of transactional relationships.

Very few people are mouse in both the places or lions everywhere.

Eighty per cent unfortunately are lions at home and mouse outside although those relationships outside are not really permanent. Their own people suffer while others outside elect them as leaders and idols. There is a twenty per cent chance that who is a lion to the world outside; who is seen snaring at different people; calls a spade a spade and is ruthless with decisions; is in fact the most attached and loving person at home. Perhaps they have realised far early what's the most precious treasure one can have and are carefully guarding and loving that treasure - their family each and every day of their life. The fans may be nonexistent or few. Perceptions may be in shambles but in sickness and good health – in ups and downs – in happiness or in sorrow these lions that roam the wide jungles are the ones who you can count on.

My notes: On Life Skills / Management and Leadership

If you've run out of page space – You are Gutching!

Bikram hollered a good deal more

1. Everybody needs to manage stress effectively. There is no one method that applies to all. We are owners of our own routes for rejuvenation. If children and pets work for you, then channelize yourself to spend time with them, if exercise or yoga it is then be regimented. But note that sanctity of mind is maintained by allowing the mind to heal each day after burning it with overtime duty.

2. Children are little bold people. They throw signs at you for seeking your company. Your alertness will tell you they want YOU to break the ice and find them. Adults, many times, operate just like children waiting for someone else to take the lead and approach them however showing signs they want to be sought. You have the choice to ignore them, or respond. Seeking them out will possibly throw pleasant surprises; at times refreshing your mind in that moment or adding a new friend to life.

3. Surreptitious rendezvous and engrossing conversations are fun not matter how simple and what the differences are between those in such dialogue.

4. We don't have to necessarily judge the intelligence of our company all the time. It is when we don't judge that we find intelligent people come in small sizes, small places and small ages too.

5. Each of us is being speculated by others just as we are speculating - the assumptions and judgments we make is out of old habit. A habit formed by prehistoric man perhaps, to assess traits of potential enemy, danger and possible confrontations. The primary aim of just evaluations is plain and simple self-preservation.

6. The first thing we look for in someone we have just met is HOW SAFE ARE THEY to be around.

7. Trust building is over complicated as subjects in management and leadership programs. A big part of trust comes from comfort and sense of safety. How a person appears, what their expressions look like, body language, eyes and smile say a lot. When you don't have your own guard up, others sense it. One who has no visible guard is one who is considered safe — because they are not ready to spar.

8. We may live in a civilized society with learnt behaviors and conduct but the innate animal instinct in us is subconsciously reading signs all the time. The real reason why life has become complicated is because of the external coating and superficiality that modern lifestyles have thrust upon us. The mind and behavior need not always tally.

9. A few bad experiences with that and we automatically become suspicious of people who are overly aggressive, imagining, "If they are so dangerous on the outside, imagine how they will be when you get to know them."

10. People who are less filtered about their conduct usually care less about opinions and perspectives. Their rawness will attract only those who like fluidity of emotions. You get what you see. The one good thing you can expect from such honest people is less hypocrisy. Please note: We are not referring to people with anger management issues, social derelicts and those suffering from personality disorders or proven record of destructive aggression.

11. Some people actually like and are drawn to such overtly tough people. Either to sharpen their own skills or because they enjoy brutal frankness and are tired of living among people who are phonier than cheap plastic.

12. Most others with weaker self-confidence stay away from those demonstrating overtly robust character because they are unsure if they are adept at handling so much rawness.

13. Normally the rejection of a person with overt aggressiveness is on account of an expression mismatch. I don't express like that and I would prefer to be with those who I can predict and are more like me.

14. What spooks us, rankles our balance or disturbs our demeanor is avoidable.

15. We read people continuously and not just at the first glance. You meet someone who offers a toothy grin, warm handshake and enquires about you listening intently and they pass gate one. But the mind is still working at the lunch-table looking for any contradictions to assessments that cleared gate one. They have many friends, people who appear to like them, listen to others the same way, shows respect – Cleared gate two. But now you hear a credit card collection call and they snap. Didn't answer to their mother's call. Yelled at a steward and they don't tally with anything you approved them of. The mind warns they behave as per social status, ranking and use of a person. Now your mind rings the alarm and you place the person outside the first gate. This is how we process safety.

16. Some equations are so long running yet we see our mind watching, assessing and announcing deviations, years after you think you should know someone. This is because people are continuously evolving. You perhaps don't acknowledge it but your sub conscious mind has tracked changes in people and behavior which is why it gate keeps close to seven years into knowing someone.

17. A lot of our first level feeder is also hearsay. What others say. Some are weaker than others which is why such information becomes gospel truth and they

turn into poor judge of people.

18. The smallest and most insignificant seeming people are usually the owners of grapevines. They add fuel to fires. Often taking the liberty to also sketch caricatures as they please if only to infuse drama in their storytelling.

19. What gets repeated to ten people – becomes reputation and also perception.

20. We all suffer from self-fulfilling prophesies, where we want our assessments to be proven to be true. So if we judge someone to be disloyal or a fraud for instance, the mind is consciously searching for all or any data to stick to that judgment thus adding weight to claim; giving you a boost in confidence…that you are indeed a good judge of people.

21. The clearer and more objective a person is, the more distance they keep from social noise, gossip and small talk.

22. They are usually guided by their own systems, values and beliefs not requiring confirmations and approvals from others to be who they want to be.

23. The flip side of such enigmatic yet aggressive leadership trait is that their dominance and confidence could be misunderstood for lack of human concern and insensitivity.

24. The more cocky and conceited our assessments about others; the more is the tendency to operate from a "Holier than thou" position. This diminishes any chance of breaking glass walls because interactions will get fewer and the viewing glass a narrowing jaundiced one.

25. This goes to prove that it is important for people in leading positions at work to reach out and not allow others to make assumptions. The duty of interaction lies with the leader.

26. For leaders for whom wrong image and assumptions are "just water off a ducks back"; such nonchalance works for them temporarily. Because they have created an insulation, it won't cause sleepless nights; but in the long run the divide between people and self will become a chasm. If business and results are important, then people matter. Their minds matter. And your reputation as a leader matters… so they feel like following you.

27. Most often revelations happen, curtains rise and walls break during a crisis, or conflict or because the relationship has neared an end. This is the period when people hold honest conversations revealing what they really think, feel, see and experience.

28. At times people are too shy to accept mistakes of judgment, concede to their own folly which is why they allow good people and good relationships to die.

EGO - the biggest relationship killer!

29. Good counsel can come from odd places. We don't need to sift people by age, education, place and culture for advice.

30. Kind people don't make a show and dance of their giving. Real charity is humble and quiet, with no expectation for anything in return.

31. A true giver makes the decision to stand up and be a better human being, not because of any incentive except the joy of doing something that feels right.

32. Causes that people get attached to, begin to direct and consume energy. It becomes a very private driving force. Those engrossed in such causes find it hard to consider the company of others who cannot fathom or respect it.

33. Character, behavior, and manners are best evaluated when a person is under stress. Like the child who was in control of his emotions despite being fraught in worry over food and safety – who still came to meet Bikram to return his belongings; like the two kids who helped him about the house to pay off in small ways for his kindness – there will be moments ample to check real nature.

34. People who operate out of higher value for human life and human rights have low tolerance for wrongdoing and unethical actions in general. They bring that sense of propriety to all aspects of their lives.

35. Courage comes from knowing you are doing the right thing. That confidence is what prevents you from worrying about consequences too much.

36. Not all people we see as brusque, rude and aggressive need be unsuccessful in their personal life. Such people often compartmentalize their own attitude and actions...saving the best of themselves for those they love. What appears hard and calloused for outsiders could be hiding tender and amiable version visible only for their loved ones.

37. This means the reverse would also apply. Who appears tender and amiable could be roguish and selfish to the core, making other people's life miserable. Which is why perceptions fail and disillusionment is so common.

38. Strength of a person with a mission in life lies in having found someone or some people who believe in them. The unfaltering pillar of support is often why people fall, stand, run, fall stand and run again.

39. Partners are any two people with a conspicuous, celebrated unison that spells common goals coherently while defending and protecting each other's interests every day.

(Did you get all 39 observations or have you started beating this list now?)

Story 7
Catch the Ball!

On drawing inspiration, remembering to apply, learning from others and evolution

Sometimes your own life is a good teacher; provided you pause to reckon its teachings. And when you don't synthesize it as you should – will come some events and people who make it explicit for you. Catch the ball people throw…don't wait for life to throw it in your face.

This last story comes from my own youth. It would be incomplete without a walk through some of my circumstances at the time.

My father, K.W. Raghunath was a portrayal of non-conservative thinking; for an age and time when India was cocooned and our society was rather narrow-minded. He wasn't liberal when it came to freedom and socializing permits for girls but on careers, conversations, independence and exploration he was way ahead of his times. Dad traveled around India in uniform, serving the Indian Air Force for many years and scaled every place, NWSE there is. His passion would be evident in how he connected and related to strangers, even foreigners regardless of color, race or faith. In fact there would be no difference in how he related to someone at the government office, a street vendor, a CEO or a foreigner. Very early on, I learnt people are the same – it depends on how you look at them. One day I asked him about the differences we apparently display, he antiseptically said, "We are all biodegradable and in that is placed the common thread that binds us all."

The people he met were an advancement to his life experiences. Dad was a storyteller. Often, he would narrate his own stories to people or other people's stories that accelerated his ability to convince his listeners. He was an established influencer. My father, whose stories laced with lessons learned from people, realization from events, messages from strangers mesmerized everyone, enthralled me the most. Eventually it inspired me to look at travel beyond just the means of seeing places. All biologically functional set of eyes can do that. What are you doing extraordinarily as you travel, as you live? I started keeping travel notes because of him. He encouraged me to keep a diary. It helped me extrapolate from them, what I gathered walking around places — meeting new faces. I am a chip of the old block in many ways, just newer stories to tell and some offbeat view on things. But I owe my 'all seeing eyes', 'all hearing ears' and ability to talk to anyone to DAD.

It was 1995 and I had just completed college, majoring in Human Development at SNDT Mumbai, at the age of nineteen. My parents put me in school when I was in the pram I guess, so graduation was completed two years ahead of most others my age. I struggled all my years of formal education with pronounced ADHD (Attention Deficit Hyperactivity Disorder). ADHD gave me energy that is otherwise found in a fusion reactor. So childhood was a social chaos. Normal people with precious articles in beautifully kept homes were petrified to have me visiting. To make my early life's canvas one big blurry mess — I was also slowed down by a stifling case of Dyslexia. We are talking 1976 to 1995 when India was submerged in still fixing the economy and poverty issues. Nobody cared why some kid could not write or produce in pen what she said perfectly well.

The years of structured education, with rote learning and vomiting the textbook lines in the same order was hell's format for me. It fried my grey cells, fumigating the last iota of natural interest possible. I was seriously holding on to education, with a fight. Nobody in India knew the existence of learning disorders at the time, so those unable to score well were categorically told they were idiots, or are lazy, or just useless, or were going to be the next servants of India. Pretty much, that was the assessment and prophecy for my future as well. Dim I say. Having heard the crystal ball gazing around my tomorrow, I was keen to get off on any station rather than land where they all said I would. On some hard days, I earnestly prayed for the holocaust to be arranged so I would be out of this crappy creek my life was left meandering in.The escapist in me always looked for exit routes.

Which is why I ran away with Winston Churchill the first time I read his lines that confirmed most of his education happened outside of school. I held it to my bosom and promised him *I will continue his legacy. I will not make sure Churchill does not see my face at any post grad college convocation, as long as I live.*

With that solemn promise I also had to promise my new found guru, that I will be just like him — I will learn from the roads and bylanes of life, each day; never missing the chance to grow personally and professionally. My sword will be sharper than anyone who used a whetstone. My mind and tongue shall swagger and slash anyone who attempts to stand in my way, compelling me to follow traditional routes for building knowledge and intelligence. His soul must have been pretty pleased to note such fanship existed. Churchill was my guide, philosopher and muse for long. His own relationship with India was far from impressive but I had compartmentalized the aspect that impressed me from what did not. When situations went out of hand, I ran to Winston Churchill quotes. Inevitably, he would have left me a witty, snappy, breezy quote that elevated me out of my down-time and gave me the zip to go fix it. My journey unto self-learning had begun. No hill was too tall for me with Churchill.

The man had a brusque side to personality. He was known to be a rogue leader as well. Not inclusive, not sensitive to people and had flaws in his being like many leaders and most people have. But when we choose a muse the most protrusive part of their characteristics have to satisfy your gap or developmental need. I wasn't sassy enough as a growing teenager. I had the self-esteem of the Twin Towers after they were razed to the ground. Same potential, same might and same ability to have created possibilities. I was ruined by callous, malevolent others who terrorized and brought me down to shambles. There was zero confidence, sub zero esteem and no strength to protect myself. I knew there was a need to be sharp, so that the world couldn't devour me. Who else but Churchill to teach sassy!

In the last year of graduation, Dad was diagnosed with stomach cancer. It was the last stage and he hardly had time to live. Nine months to a year at the maximum, the cold-hearted doctor had predicted like he was reading the expiry date of a jam or bottle of sauce. I hated doctors that day on. A job where you have to spell out the shelf life of a person for a living and to pick that profession by choice! Loss of my father in such a gruesome way had disrupted perceptions about the entire medical fraternity. Over the years, after overcoming my father's death, I have become more accommodating of doctors as a profession. Today, I see doctors as brave people who embrace a career life among platelets, IVs, stories of death, and gory sights because someone has to do it and cowards like me run the other way. Maturity bobs its head in the aftermath of strong emotions.

The doctors did their best and we spent a fortune in treatment over the two years. Hospitals, operations, nursing, chemo — it had drained the bank as much as it had drained Dad. I was determined not to be a burden to the family at a time like this. Under normal circumstances my parents would have sent me packing to study some more and stretch my term in another education prison somewhere. Now with weak financial disposition, that scary possibility was ruled out, I could not stay unproductive and parasitic. So I went in search of a job. There was a giant company in India that was commencing a "jewelry retail concept". It was going to revolutionize the way this gold hungry community purchased and invested in the yellow metal from there on. This rich organization was hiring young people. They sought talent with some experience. I had none. In the requisites, they wrote strong in communication skill as a must. The candidate has to be confident and a quick learner. I was a far cry from all that but I was desperate and applied anyway. I was competing with talent who had experience and those that has connections too. I have no clue how I made it, but I did and think it was pure benevolence that graced upon me such an outcome.

It was ray of tepid happiness after many days of the over cloud that Dad's illness brought upon us. At least I could go home and tell my family they didn't have to worry about me dragging feet or being a liability. Better still, in some time I will actually be contributing. Dad was elated, despite his weakness and wafer-thin body. Then I broke the news that I will have to go to Bangalore and be parked there for twenty odd days; that's the amount of time the training program will take. I had a sinking feeling that my overprotective Dad will cringe. He was born allergic to the word "boys". He would imagine roads and offices filled with two-legged lanky, cheeky boys nudging his precious daughter and instantly reject my request for permission. I could see him visualizing just that but his disease was compelling him to allow me some liberation. So I got a yes from him and also had to make all kinds of promises; most of which appeared totally fictional events to me. But I had to calm down a sick man and give him as much comfort as I could, so I agreed I won't be too modern (whatever that meant), no partying and no staying out late (like as if I ever went to one) I had no idea what clubs looked like or what socials were. Had no skills to demonstrate anything at a club even if by accident I landed there– didn't dance, didn't sing – the one "—ing" word I did well was nothing. We were raised like colorfully dressed nuns at a nunnery and he was telling me not to be too forward!

That struck me, I was going to travel alone. I was going to meet fresh faces, stay in an uncontrolled environment. Be allowed to talk and mingle without feeling my father's frown upon my back. It felt promising. On the trip, I met a bunch of girls – all newly recruited by the company. I was never shy. Being an avid sports enthusiast, some bit of lively zest was kept alive but I was the kind of shy that comes from not having social ranking. The one in India you earn from being a merit ranker or for being born into money. When money is sparse and pains are several, there is a kind of reticence that comes over many and I was suffering from that badly. It strips off your cool quotient and makes you worry — what if the others choose to do things that your jingling pockets will not allow? I was raised in much comfort and had a more than a satisfying, childhood. But Dad's cancer was about four-five years old. While he was diagnosed late he had been ill for long. He had stopped working while sick and undiagnosed. We were not used to penny pinching, yet there we were, learning to adjust to a thinner wallet. With strong resolve that I will not succumb to any such peer pressure and keep to myself, I allowed that journey to unfold.

There was a mean "Cat Woman" there among the new recruits who took an instant dislike towards me. She was minus the black suit and good work but all cat. At the first sight of me she immediately decided that I will be the reception point of all her viciousness. Interestingly she had visible whiskers that grew on her upper lip and that made the catty theme come alive for me. Every time she got nasty I would stare at her whiskers and it gave me some comfort that heaven was not hundred per cent in her favor. This bit may have been my cattiest side. But nothing mean enough to put her in place would ever escape my mouth. No matter how hard I wanted to put a cork on her foul mouth and sick attitude, I wasn't smart-mouthed. I was petrified at how someone can be so predatory and downright classless, yet get away with it all the time. But that is how Alpha girls can be, who propel themselves on daddy's money, daddy's contacts and daddy's friends and it is daddy who also gives them their jobs. I had a dad who was fighting to live just another day — this war was going to be hard. But it would force me to grow up too – I could tell that much.

She looked like she was trying hard to win the "Venom of the Century" award. I doubt if there would have been any competition worthy of her forked tongue anywhere in the world. She was dipped in the liquid green of money when she was born and reeked of its smell in the designer bags she carried, clothes and shoes she wore or even pens in her side pocket. She made it a point to mention what brands they were so "Hey! Pass the bag!" wouldn't be just about the bag – it would be, "Hey! Pass me my Prada!"

We are talking of India over twenty years ago when cable TV was only five years old. English sitcoms - Ninety five percent of the country could not follow. When western music sounded like a whole lot of screaming into a mike and soap operas like Santa Barbara and Bold and Beautiful were considered morally dismembering. We were stuck in a beautiful Indian-ness at the time that had not fused with the idea of Global citizen yet.

Internet had not opened doors to the world outside. Pagers were common but the mobile had not made its ground-shaking appearance. And there she was, name-throwing foreign cities she had traveled to and food she loves from a quaint village in Denmark or the best hotdog stand in California…all that sounded like gibberish to everyone else. But Sonia made everyone's life miserable and if that was a paying job, she would have earned overtime each day. She made a few favorites, like most Alphas do. These were the flunky variety ever Alpha male or female carries. The kind that suck up to gain favors like entry into a uppity party, all-paid-for-dinner , the chance to hitch a ride in a fancy car they can only dream about and so on. Flunkies are soul sellers. They give their soul away for a free milkshake!

I observed there was me and another girl Bindu who didn't fan her ego that was the size of a giant gas balloon. So there in Bindu, I found a self-respecting human being and we immediately latched on to support my theory "There is safety in numbers". It is not a figment of imagination. It is reality. Alone you will be outnumbered. With company, it gets harder to get hunted. At least there will be a witness during the kill. My eyes were opening up to realities of harsh adult life by the minute. Bindu was a couple of years older than me and had worked before. She had some experience with nuisance like this, so she ignored most of it and seemed to be cool as a cucumber while I fretted and fumed uncontrollably. I was envious of Bindu's calm but couldn't speed up to catch up with her Buddha lotus pose.

We reached Bangalore. By that time, I had become Bindu's under wing. She was brave and bold. If need be, she will swing her purse on this bubble head was my conviction. We rushed to the hotel reception desk to ensure we would be staying together. But luck was not to be. However we were placed close by and I found respite in that assurance. We dined together and shared notes on what we observed about our pet mutual hate. Lot of hooliganism and bullying. But there was nothing we could do about it. We spent the next two days testing waters gently with others who came from other cities. Many hated the sight of Sonia. That's when I noticed my protector was as ruffled by her as I was. So if things got ugly we both will be out in the sun. The catty girl decided to make us her prime target. Because we would not go "Hail Sonia" – her warehouse of snide remarks under the belt lines, jabs at style, dressing – whatever — was showered upon us without a filter. Over time the suckers grew and almost all others moved to her camp and it was just Bindu and me. We were not informed of evening plans, of dinner hours or when they would leave in the morning. We were social rejects and that became evident in how cold the environment suddenly got to be.

We were quite relieved at being left out, frankly. That terminated unwanted exposure. Bindu and I laughed like we were on weed all the time. In retrospect I think it was partially because of anxiety — not knowing when will come the next attack and some parts because we found it hilarious that two such examples of feminine brilliance were being stacked in a reject list. Bindu and I decided to make the most of the next fifteen days we had there. Central park was a lovely hotel to stay in and the Orange country served an awesome breakfast each morning. Evenings, Bindu and I would make plans to go for walks, shop nearby, eat a small meal some place…again laugh at out plight or in unison, gripe about the pain in our life. That was our bonding connect. Sonia threw us together and we just ended up being great friends there on. Deep down, I had wild spunk that frightened Bindu sometimes and she feared I will go out of hand and break some protocol the day I find my bearings. She had decent sixth sense, I say!

Bindu's prediction came true a few months later; when I gave a Martin Luther styled speech on equality, respect and fairness right there — on the work floor. It covered work ethics, dignity of labor and human rights impromptu fueled only by passion. The lecture was targeted at the diabolical woman owner who was a photocopy of Sonia in a blown up size. Birds of a feather flock together. Made sense why she got a job here. They were all a set who knew each other personally. But the owner of the Franchise store was a tyrant who ran the place like a sweat shop. I had enough of Sonia and enough of her.

My speech had Bindu cracking all her fingers at once with nervousness. I think the whole combination of a nasty peer in Sonia and her adult version for a storeowner just sprung a loose connection in my spark plug. The showroom was more like a high society circus and not a workplace at all. She was running slave under the whip that didn't tally with company norms or policies. Being a society page three character's wife, she thought employees were yesterday's garbage. Bunch of purchased servants. That speech was my peace offering to her and the Sonia's kind. I quit that night and gave that job the boot it deserved. My innocuous speech was delivered at a potent decibel, in chaste eloquent English; which apparently had that office reverberating in for weeks to come. It was something people of their denomination will remember in their next lives to come as well because of how hard I shoved it into the memory of their DNA's soul.

Too many people unwell in the mind can make any sane person lose their equilibrium. Bindu had picked up this no-nonsense side of me and also the dormant wild horse courage that was rather juvenile in those days. Truth is it was made volcanic by a chance meeting. That side of me was discharged by someone we met during the trip to Bangalore at Park Central - the place we lived. He was who breathed air into a splinter that I was. He flamed up that was anyway wanting its output. The scared, timid, weak side of me died forever. A new outspoken, bold and fire brand version was born. This side had courage as big as a cornfield. It got reined in later in the years and sits calm now for most parts with the potential for eruption only if situations so demand. In time I became the voice of equality, ethics, compliance, human rights, leadership, and conservation. Not just because of how fundamental they are as subjects – but because they compliment my spirit. I do owe it to him who poked me into accepting this side of my personality.

One night, during the training period while still at the hotel, Bindu and I went to have dinner at a small restaurant. We were saving pennies to get rich. Our snack/meal arrived and eyes caught a tall – seriously tall, white guy about twenty-five years old, sitting on a bench, far in the back. He was looking at us chatting and laughing while we kept a close watch on him too. He and us – we were the only decent folk in that place no matter how immodest that sounds. We had a unspoken connection for being the same type — odd. Bindu thought he was American and I guessed he was European. This argument went on for a bit and I challenged her to go ask him. She felt awkward to go up to a stranger and ask questions around domicile. I had refused to go. No guts. So a doubtful, rather awkward Bindu walked over to him with the grace of an octopus and asked him where he was from and that we had a bet. Smirking ear to ear she came back and I didn't need to know that I had lost. He was American.

Dinner done, we began walking to the hotel which was at least a twenty-minute walk. The road was dark and lonely as well. Lined with electric lamps without bulbs! Showpieces to fool people in the day. We heard footsteps behind us and there was Mr. Longfellow right behind us. On roads like that, you feel like a midget, real quick. Five feet six inches and that was neither helping her nor me. We quickened pace and he was still there. We panicked for a bit. Was that American following us? Whatever the turn of the road – he was like a shadow we couldn't shake off.

Then he called out to us and my blood curdled. This is what my dad had warned about and I am going to pay the price for not listening. He came walking faster and stopped right ahead. "If you girls think I am following you – trust me, I am not. I just happen to be heading the same way." Phew that was a relief! We giggled as hysterically as to-be-murdered-people do, when they get released on a whim. We admitted that the thought had crossed our minds. That we had indeed, thought the worst of him. And then he offered to walk with us so the real potential attackers won't think we were alone. We welcomed that chivalrous offer and soon discovered he was a guest at Central Park too. How lovely! That walk became a chatty one and we shared introduction bits as fast as we could — literally turn by turn. It was a funny walk. He was walking and both of us were jogging. Each of his strides was two or three steps for us. Bindu and I talked of Mumbai — our hometown, our new jobs, the training, the trouble we had with some girls and why we are lost lambs. With all this talking and panting, we reached the hotel.

Scott Rozic was his name. He was about twenty-six – just a few years older but decades older than me in terms of maturity — something I was going to learn in the next few days. Scott was in India to research and study India's promise on affordable talent and business operations. He had started a software company in San Francisco and wanted to hire strong software engineers to develop some products for him from Bangalore. At the time all he was talking about seemed like the language from the lost city of Atlantis for me. Too complex. But he was excited, energetic and very enthusiastic. Scott's personality was bright, chirpy and also quiet at the same time. He would light up when he talked about work. He was a visionary and that much my immature brain could assess. There he was, this young boy — stranger to my eyes…but he was strumming a song of hope, of dreams and possibilities, coming to a country like India when most of the west thought Indians have to fight a tiger or unwind a snake on the way to work each day.

Scott had no inhibitions when it came to trials and tests. He came here not knowing what the finds will be. He said he didn't have much money but to make money one has to bet some place and try real hard. This was his attempt at starting a business and see if India could be a support system that augments his concept. We found this tall guy safe, fun and really strong as a person. That evening instead of heading back to the rooms which sheltered us from the hunter called Sonia, we plopped on the seats at the reception and exchanged stories, shared information, gave view points and it was like we knew each other for the longest time. The clock ticked twelve and we knew it was getting late. We bid Scott goodnight with the promise to meet him for breakfast the next day.

He was punctual and again at the breakfast table, we began the chattering of three new-to-each-other people. We were making the most of this journey. Scott was an all American guy raised by a very loving mother, I could tell, because he was attached to home, to family and talked of them just as we did about ours. In one day, I realized American or Indian — we are a product of what our family does to us. He was raised by bold parents who encouraged and egged him to live his dream, regardless of the results. I was raised by a non-classist, equality respecting father, so there was no prejudice against Scott for being a color I didn't meet often. Bindu was raised by a father who had tremendous social skills and who accepted people as they came. And look what happened! Some parts of what our parents were was what we were carrying at the tea tables and the post dinner walks. A part of their philosophies that we had accepted well, that allowed us to accept each other.

It didn't take Scott long to realize we were doing nothing really to call evenings meaningful. Mostly because we were scared to venture out alone and explore Bangalore. He researched on good restaurants and also identified a pub we should go to. He was going to show us our first discotheque. My father's hologram was standing akimbo glaring at me but I wished him good retreat and agreed to join Scott and Bindu. The next few evenings were filled with great company, arguments, culture sharing, enquiry on one day in the life of being Scott…family orientations, beliefs, practices, likes and dislikes and with the entire spectrum covered, I felt like I had been to America. We played Scott some Indian songs, sang some English numbers, displayed foolery that would qualify with an A-grade (the kind my report card never saw). The entertainment was awesome primarily because he was receptive and most willing to tolerate however nonsensical our idea of fun was. Scott was a guy who didn't judge, who didn't hold reservations and didn't have dogmatic views.

It was easy to get along with him, like he was an amoeba and so were we, and with that we just fitted into the shape to take. Friendships built like that which don't enforce a certain template are very fulfilling. Scott taught me a lot on that trip. On how to gun for your ideas. To be calm on the surface and be paddling like a mad duck under the water. He was a businessman in the making and he was taking the plunge relying on his abilities to struggle alone. Scott was great with people. He could communicate with anyone. And people liked him. From the doorman at the hotel, a rickshaw driver, club bouncer, just about everyone could acknowledge his quiet strength. There was one club we mustered to go to one night. Some black boys went out of hand and were getting too dangerous for any of our appetites. This was a mixed race club in Bangalore that I much later learnt had a bad reputation on drugs and peddling. They were five or six that had gone rogue. We had common sense to see Scott can't handle that many. I was scared stiff into rigor mortis. Scott was fazed and for the first time I noticed the calm leave him. He quickly pushed us out towards the exit door and became the wall that separated Bindu and me from the wild crowd. We ran out like liberated refugees heaving, puffing and completely cold in skin.

I asked Scott how is that he got worried. He said courage to start a business, to go to unknown countries alone, to meet strangers and make new friends is one thing; but to extend that courage to all facets and cut-copy-paste guts will not make it courage. That is stupid bravery. Bravery is not supported by any logic or sense. There is a good chance you will go down. Discretion is the better part of valor is finally demonstrated and was not just an idiom for me. We sat down with some juices to ease the nerves. Scott loved Indian food and was more than happy to try out everything we would recommend. The friendship was as good as it can be on such a trip that short.

Xmarksthespot was his company that would soon come to life. One day I asked him what he plans to do to grow the company and his response took me aback. He wanted to grow the company, to sell it! Twenty years ago, I don't recollect hearing anyone build anything to sell. He had bigger plans and this was his stepping stone. Astounded, I realized who I had met. A maverick. Gut instinct told me he will do well with Xmarksthespot and whatever else he touches, so long as his spirit does not change.

I was stuck in life, lost, tired, weak by circumstances, controlled and very bleak in my view of what my life could be. He was like a slap on my face. He woke me up with boiling water. Scott was my diametric opposite. And it was such a pleasure to meet and see at close quarters what that other side would look like — if I took the effort to face the tide and cross the river.

The parting had to come. It was time for us to go. With a heavy heart, we bid Scott goodbye. Promised to stay in touch. For a year or so there was some communication and then it stopped. Travelers are like ships at high seas — who stop to say warm Ahoy there — and then each, sail off to their destinations. Many years later, I found Scott on LinkedIn and we connected there. He is one of my fourteen thousand connections today and we don't really communicate. But he is special. Difference is, he is the one who changed my life without knowing it. I could never erase that chance meeting with Scott. He was the dose of medicine I needed to pull up my socks to change. I had to get bolder. I had to stand up for what is right and what is good for me. The show down, ticket free drama I had staged at the uppity showroom was also a result of being inspired by Scott. He would never stand being treated with disrespect as a low grade citizen. Scott was conscious of people's space and rights. He never stepped on people's feet and wouldn't let them do that either. Churchill was given notice. I had taken on Scott as my new muse to grow with.

There on Scott became a ghost in my memory. At times, meeting him seemed unreal too. But Bindu was an equal shareholder of that meeting with the messiah. She was witness to vet his existence. Scott stayed a tenacious influence. I took wild chances with starting a business at the age of twenty-one. I set up a staffing and training company in Mumbai and successfully ran that for eight years. When my business would see a dip, I would sip some tea and think of all the energizing conversations with this lava man. He was a potent leader. Burning with ideas, plans and strategies. He drove himself to do all that he envisaged even if he had to do it alone. That is one thing that I have stayed undeterred from – a very Scott attitude to lift things up myself and run with it alone if I have to. It brought me much good repute over the years at the workplace.

I owe him much for shaping my attitude and perspectives on life, work and leadership. Scott showed me how right it is to follow your heart. Why it is important to program the mind to compliment the heart. And why energy is a must for someone with an ambitious mind. He stayed fit. Looked like a professional athlete although he didn't run for a profession but his fitness was remarkable. He stayed nimble agile and flexible to respond to the demand the career would make. He never changed on this subject even in the years to come. Scott taught me two valuable lessons for leadership excellence – the importance of courage and character which are the fulcrum of leadership.

In his company we had become the envy of the group. There were forty mouths wagging about us and our new friend. Scott would not be seen without us and we were deliriously happy learning, sharing and growing in the highly stimulating conversations. I for one changed forever. Scott had no idea how much I was learning outside of school and how he had become the guru I was worshiping. Shukriya Scott!

Seema (19) - Scott (26) and Bindu (22) - Dinner one night after a very long and winding day… learning even when bushed!

My notes: On Life Skills / Management and Leadership

If you've run out of space – You are Gutching!

Scott left much back in India

1. You can be bored and annoyed by some habits your parents have because they probably subjected you to hours of tolerating it when you were young and there was no escaping it. Yet as adults you would have turned into being a mirror image of them on some habits or skills without planning on it.

2. If you have taken after some habits and ways of your parents it means you had enough time to observe them consciously. And subconsciously your mind is picking up the merit in it. Example: I found my father's hand of friendship to all and sundry irritating. The talking to strangers — strange. And then later as an adult saw the merit of picking that up when I was ready to. Work and travel was throwing people at me. Connecting came naturally. I didn't have practice but had enough practice watching it from the stands.

3. Learnt traits are those that one acquires by formally being coached, trained and mentored in. Pre-programmed traits are those one has a natural flair for owing to high exposure to them. Not all will be selected. What comes from clear choice, becomes prominent skill. Strangely what is clear choice is not an awareness for the individual. Unless you really sit down and make notes of what you picked from who and why. The cause, the motivation and the muse becomes apparent,

4. How will you know what can be selected? Traits you see in your parents, grandparents, inspiring others need not rub off right away. It has to appeal to your spirit and who you are becoming for some facets of theirs to draw your attention.

5. Confidence is as much an internal reckoning as it is about some events or paraphernalia that aid it becoming evident.

6. Confidence is NOT a singular element with no dependence. In fact, there are several dependents and supporting lines for confidence.

7. Once confidence is discovered, it does not mean it is permanent. It requires perpetual management and protection.

8. Nobody is immune to environment unless the mind belongs to a sociopath or has mastered stoicism through delinking from community and society.

9. It is fine to know and acknowledge your vulnerability. The fact that your confidence is vacillating and truly shakes your earth sometimes is testament – you are still working on yourself.

10. It is important you note what usually causes disruption in your confidence. Note the type of people, events and conditions that ruffle your feathers. Not that any of those can be completely prevented by listing them - but it can serve as a foghorn of what is to come from within you in response and that can be altered or

be prepared for.

11. Each person operates differently when weak and not at their fighting best. Some hole up. Some will try to stand but tell the world they are wounded. That may earn sympathy but they will never really manage to inch up their confidence to deal with happenings. There are others who will give it a good fight come what may, they estimate what will be pitfalls, to avoid them consciously thereby prevent the depletion of energy further. Some prefer to keep their trauma under wraps.

12. Too much information in the wrong hands can be a mistake. To share and to relieve the burden of worry one needs to find TRUST in the listener.

13. When values match, when there is common like and dislike, when there is shared ethics – trust comes easier.

14. Independence is at times a result of cultural pressure, demand from expectation, upbringing, a need or even fear of loss. At other times it is an inbuilt program, or a slow evolution of readiness that directs a person to find their ground. It is important to know what was and is your push in life?

15. Involuntary entry into early independence brings an abrupt change of environment that demands new behaviors and maturity. People who have been through this grind have another color to their prism that comes from many more years of ownership and accountability.

16. Death and disease is debilitating to a family who has to watch a loved one proceed to their fatalistic end. This is the weakest point of human life – watching someone die. A person who is a nurturer or in any form protector/support giver is in an emotional and spiritual havoc. But the rest of the world moves at its normal pace. Managing this equilibrium is the hardest for them because others don't understand. This is the period we need to offer our most considerate side to those going through this phase.

17. However it would be impractical to expect sensitivity or kindness from people who are not by nature civil, non-competitive, concerned and humane. Your moment of downtime is perhaps their time to shine. It is okay to not be in charge of life all the time. At times just go with the way the day wants to unfold. As long as you have the faith that you will bounce back and take charge – a temporary lull is not the end and might actually do good.

18. Whether it is financial woes or career issues, if you recognize it as testing times, there is just one thing to be cautious of – the building of an ivory tower from where everyone else looks wrong, small or not worthy of your association. This can be a defense mechanism the mind at times resorts to, to protect oneself from feeling more miserable but one that sadly ends up alienating you.

19. Just because your chips are down does not mean you need to eat humble pie, swallow insults, get humiliated, be treated poorly or tolerate wrong doing. Don't let such a phase be the time you get used to being walked over. Once a doormat always a doormat. A wounded lion – you are allowed to be. Go roam alone for a while. Lick your wounds. Heal. But when you come back – you should still be a king.

20. If circumstances weaken your stand, accept the circumstances. Your responses are adaptation to the stimulation. That need not really be who you are. You may appear meek, confused, stuck in a rut with nothing moving forward but that's not because you are weak. Expressed strength is a result of ideal conditions. When the conditions are conducive your strength too shall surface.

21. Demand your place, your rights, your ground – no one has any proprietary hold over your existence. The ability to command your place is what will make you tick.

22. As long as your view of the world and people is not jaundiced and you see things unbiased, state facts and eloquently deliver the argument, your presentation will stand the test of time. Importantly reinstate your confidence in yourself.

23. In most cases subjugation, deprivation, trauma, ill treatment happen to those who allow it. You can draw the energy from within or find your muse.

24. Befriend people with whom you feel anchored in your views, perspectives and your energy. They will make your gray skies blue.

25. Stay open to meeting new people and extend that hand of friendship – you never know what part of you they will hoist and recharge.

26. At times, people we meet will appear to be nowhere close to understanding your disposition and seem to be living in a parallel universe where everything is smooth sailing. That dichotomy should be your magnet. Attach yourself to people not moaning – not deflated – not curbed. It will levitate your being.

27. If you listen and watch closely people with dreams, some of their madness and positive thinking is bound to rub off on you. They are opportunity seekers, optimists to the zenith.

28. A dreamer never rests and in their company you could find the revitalizer you need.

29. It would be best when you reckon a constant buzz of energy. Drive stays with only those who have clear dreams, goals and destinations. When they achieve what they wanted – a new one is crafted before the previous one dies. Passion is reborn in new shapes and forms. But never dies out. Find the meaning that will be the driving force. It's okay to be driven and running all the time it's any day better

than to stagnate.

30. Learning from someone means truly valuing what they came to teach. The best way to imbibe is to apply immediately. Do not wait for the constellations to come together and continents to collide for the opportune time. Being able to demonstrate what you learnt will allow you to handle the repercussions of your well thought through actions and deal with what corrections need to be taken as soon as possible.

31. Dilly-dallying learners will not progress. Fear prevents application. Most learning is wasted on people who give programs great ratings, follow an inspiring someone, post other people's quotes, give great feedback – and then do nothing about it to make it their own. You DO NOT own your learning until you DO it. Best to ACT on it, in quick succession to the acceptance of a learning.

32. Courage is key. To learn, to grow, to do and to change. At time courage may seem disruptive. But unless you try, you won't know will you? If your method or ways were obtuse, not refined, has room for improvement – you will get there the next time. But until that first forward step is taken, the rest won't follow.

33. Bravery is a dangerous thing. Just because you know your strengths in one space you can't be foolish to think it will apply to all facets of life. One can be courageous in one area but totally uncomfortable elsewhere. Knowledge of where your courage is well rooted and where it is not gives you more courage to respond in spontaneity when situations so demand.

34. Do the never done before. Break rules if you have to. Explore whatever your mind seeks. Tempt your luck. Attempt to change destiny. Take the risk. If you won't shake yourself – when time does it trust me it usually is a lot less fun. At least when you shake yourself you do it yourself, it is with your wits around. When you choose your own destiny it is in cognizance of your interests and dreams so even if you are heading without a map, it will be a joyous one.

35. If you choose to sit out life, then when you least expect it one of life's whimsical jokes will pull the rug from under your feet and since you never fell before – it will really be a hard thud. For those who try often, they fall so often that falling stops to matter.

36. Falling is very good to grow strong legs. You eventually learn how to fall. Practice the fall so you won't ever fatally get hurt. Besides those who do take chances, become so good at analyzing risk, the possible nets, the tools and back up – they actually manage to get out of situations unscathed that would have ruined many others who always played it safe.

37. Consistency of environment can make you insipid. The same organization,

the same work, the same bars, the same people, the same thinking, the same ideas and while you won't know about it you would be part of a mold where others carrying different features are just as interesting or boring as you are.

38. The one thing that still excites someone who has everything – is the potential of meeting a mind that can instigate, be a catalyst and in that be the incentive to share time and space.

39. How you accommodate and welcome people unlike yourself speaks much for your upbringing and our perception of the world.

40. Friendship is the purest form of human relationship that often has no real exchange rate except fun conversations and great company. Even the shortest of friendships can leave lasting memories.

41. Some friendships alter life and personality. They liberate you. Allow you to flower. By being themselves they pave the way for you to follow.

42. You may not meet the people who you owe much for, ever again. But you can keep them alive as mentors who will fuel your drive when you are running low.

43. Your muse has to be someone who is ample in what is your deficit. They need to be people who are naturals in the space. Nothing effectuated or synthetic. However highly pronounced in what you wish to be and learn how to be.

44. When faced with a situation that provides you a chance to be like your muse – you have to think of them and what they would do here. HOW is your call. But WHAT they would have done will help to clear up the fog on the course of action. In time you will develop your own style that is more attached to your personality.

45. The more you believe what people assume, agree with it to be the truth without exploring it on your own — you will be fastening the cork on any possibility for new adventure. Joy comes to the wild horse seen running across ranges and rivers, not the tame ones shuffling in the stables.

46. Memories are precious not because they are your memories but because some of these quantified and qualified your life.

(If you got as many observations or more ....You are Gutching!)

"The people who helped you build memories are actors in the movie of your life. You may be the star but they gave strokes to your character"

OBSERVATION...

The 3rd eye of Leadership & the passport to Natural Intelligence

Among all known competencies in Leadership, if there is one that never found glory, that was not exalted as much as it ought to have been...it is Observation skills. Natural Intelligence demands it's extensive use and mastery too. Who has cultivated Observation ability will thrive in every weather, change and also the people they meet.

Besides it is a skill that cannot be taken away once learnt. The 3rd eye is what makes one truly different from the others. It bestows unimaginable power upon it's user. In time a person who has been sharpening this skill learns to depend on it like an old friend. And it is this innate ability to know more than what is out there; to seek and find what others can't and to sense through the many signs...which makes one Naturally Intelligent. It is a non- academic intelligence that is highly transferable to any subject, domain or space of life.

As you may have realised by now - building Observation skills takes much practice. And practice lies in the most simple of life events / meetings / conversations / travels. Hopefully the 7 stories have tested your ability enough. And if you really got better towards the later stories, then you can be sure you have upped your skills while reading this book. But let this not be the end of your tinkering....you must go on with each days opportunities.

The birth of Natural Leadership hinges on Natural Intelligence and Natural Intelligence itself rests in Observation skills. The 3rd eye of Leadership is nothing less than decades of staying in practice... till it is a habit.

About the Author

Seema Raghunath is an HR professional with 23 years of experience in leading HR and Business. She began her career in Banking Sales at the age of 19 as soon as she graduated in Human Resource Development from SNDT University. Having done well in the space for 2 years she moved on to breathe life into the idea of a start-up company.

She set up a Consultancy outfit that specialized in Hiring, Training, Market study and OD activities. Being the youngest entrepreneur operating in Manpower Consulting at the time, she earned much recognition over the next 7 years. Seema came back to work as an HR professional at the age of 28 and served quite a few prestigious global and Indian brands.

After 20 years of working she decided to take a break to pursue her dream – of writing books. This passion drove her to write 5 management books within 1.5 years. Of which, 2 have been published while others are with publishers. Her first book 'The Corporate Jungle' published by HarperCollins has won accolades from employees world over. The book won The National Book Honor 2017 award under "Best book in Management". I Gutching is her second release.

Today Seema Raghunath Heads HR for a reputed Insurance brand. She is a mother to two daughters aged 21 and 20. In her spare time she writes blogs and teaches Teens about living safely. She deployed her skills as a Life coach to create self-help modules that people can leverage when in trouble. This project has won her an award in 2018 "Best HR for Society".

"The road is bumpy and maybe a wagon wheel fell off too. But for as long as the sun is roaring fine, we will get past the hurdles together… to reach the other side"

– Seema Raghunath

I Gutching is meant to wake you up; convince you to see people outside of given definitions; push you to evaluate and judge people as strong or poor talent only AFTER you give them a fair chance to fight. If your own 3rd eye is awakened… you will view the world unlike the masses and find in others what they possibly don't know of themselves. The consciousness of your mind will put to sleep all the prejudice the world has painstakingly taught you. And with that you will be the OUTLIER who has no boundaries.

Keep the eye open – the world is fusing. Geographies don't matter, color is only skin and life is only so many days. Tomorrow belongs to only those who see land with it's people and think it does not need to be conquered – it has to be savoured.

The world belongs to those who respect people without prejudice - those who don't care so much for the shrines erected over our differences; those who see people as tutors and thus destroy socially constructed divides. A sense of inflated supremacy is the ultimate fallacy of the backward; because the ones who have evolved reckon we are equals… who are biodegrable.

In a life that is transient there can be only time for celebrations….and LEARNING. The 3rd Eye changes YOU.
TO BE THE CHANGE AGENT…BE THE CHANGE !

"To make the most of your education...read, travel, think, write, talk to intelligent people from all walks of life and be courageous enough to break rules"

Other #SMBooks

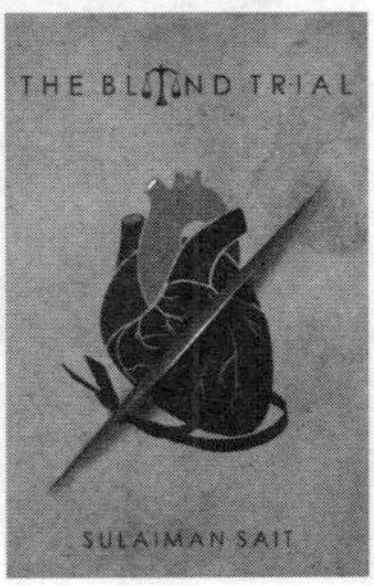

Other #SMBooks

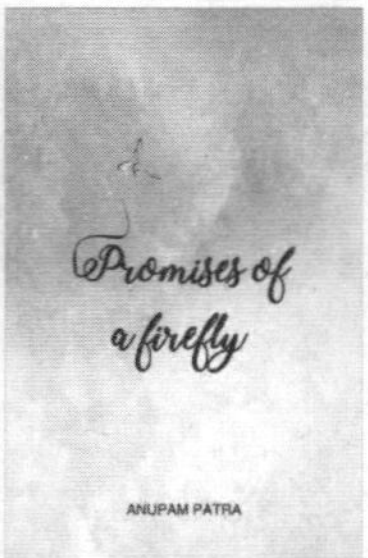